Is Russia Reformable?

Is Russia Reformable?

Change and Resistance from Stalin to Gorbachev

Robert V. Daniels

Westview Press
BOULDER & LONDON

Copyright © 1988 by Westview Press, Inc.

Published in 1988 in the United States of America by Westview Press, Inc., 5500 Central Avenue, Boulder, Colorado 80301

Library of Congress Cataloging-in-Publication Data
Daniels, Robert Vincent.
  Is Russia reformable? : change and resistance from Stalin to
Gorbachev / Robert V. Daniels.
     p.   cm.
  Includes index.
  ISBN 0-8133-0759-7
  1. Soviet Union—Politics and government—1917-   . I. Title.
DK266.D27   1988
947.084—dc19   88-15373
                                                                                    CIP

Printed and bound in the United States of America

  ∞   The paper used in this publication meets the requirements of the American National
       Standard for Permanence of Paper for Printed Library Materials Z39.48-1984.

10   9   8   7   6   5   4   3   2   1

Contents

Preface

History is always full of surprises as it unfolds before us. The Soviet Union, for decades a seemingly frozen monolith of totalitarian rigidity and paranoid bellicosity, suddenly finds itself under a leader in the person of Mikhail Gorbachev who calls for "radical restructuring," "openness," and even a "revolution." Outsiders justly wonder if this means a new era of reform, or whether the nature of the Soviet system and its historical roots makes real change impossible.

This book is based on a series of articles that I wrote during the first two years after Gorbachev assumed the Soviet leadership in March 1985. All of them attempt to get at the answer to just this question—is Russia indeed reformable? Going beyond the intentions of the leader of the moment, which may be deep or shallow, enduring or transitory, what are the forces and circumstances that demand reform on the one hand and that operate to frustrate it on the other? It is hardly necessary to underscore the importance of assessing these obstacles and possibilities as the historical record suggests them.

There are several intertwined themes running through these essays that bear on the central question of Russia's reformability. Each is the particular focus of one or more chapters, though all of these conceptions have underlain the thinking of the entire series, thereby conferring such unity as the work as a whole may show.

Underlying every chapter that follows is the proposition that Russia is still in the terminal stage of a complex revolutionary process that profoundly shaped the character of the Soviet system. This has been manifested above all, as Chapter 1 argues, in the prolonged postrevolutionary dictatorship fashioned by Stalin and bequeathed to his successors. The outcome for half a century, described in Chapter 2, was the military model of socialism that distinguished Stalinism and justifiably earned the label "totalitarian." The historical foundations in Russian political culture which underlay this militarized system and contributed to its longevity are the focus of Chapter 3. This congruence of the prerevolutionary and the postrevolutionary is not a contradiction, if the nature of the revolutionary process and its postrevolutionary phase are properly understood.

With Chapter 4 the emphasis shifts to the forces that have supported reform in the past and promote it again today. First and foremost this means the intelligentsia in all its ramifications, together with the advance of modernization that has steadily enhanced its influence. Chapter 4 focuses on the role of the intelligentsia in the reform efforts of the immediate post-Stalin period. Chapter 6 picks up this theme again with emphasis on the most recent developments. In between, Chapter 5 examines the processes and changes in the governing political system, above all the generational upheaval following the demise of Brezhnev, that offer an opening for reform. Finally, Chapter 7 explores the theme of a return to revolutionary beginnings whose realization was abnormally delayed by the failure of reform in the Khrushchev era. The import of the second half of the book is that reform in a modern society is not only possible but an economic and political imperative, demanded further by the logic of the revolution itself. These realities Gorbachev appears to have recognized. Though reform failed once, failure is now less likely.

The essays of which this book is composed were originally published in diverse journals or collections in the United States, the United Kingdom, and Italy, some in Italian translation. Five of the seven chapters are appearing for the first time in accessible English-language form. I have revised the essays only slightly for this book, to minimize repetitiveness and improve readability. No attempt has been made to update the story beyond the summer of 1987.

Chapter 1, "The Foundations of Stalinism," appeared as "The Legacy of Stalinism" in the first issue of the new Italian journal *Socialismo/Storia* (Annali della Fondazione Giacomo Brodolini, 1987), entitled "Ripensare il 1956" (Rethinking 1956, Rome: Edizioni Lerici, 1987; copyright © by Edizioni Lerici).

Chapter 2, "Lenin, Stalin, and the Military Model of Socialism," was originally prepared as a seminar paper for the Kennan Institute of Advanced Russian Studies in Washington, D.C., and issued as Occasional Paper no. 200 of the Kennan Institute under the title, "The Militarization of Socialism in Russia, 1902–1946" (1985). It was subsequently published in abridged translation as "Il socialismo da caserma" (The Socialism of the Barracks) in *Mondoperaio*, May 1986 (copyright © 1986 by Mondoperaio Edizioni Avanti!). I am grateful to the Kennan Institute for its support and to Dorothea Hanson for expert research assistance on this project.

"Stalinism and Russian Political Culture," Chapter 3, was prepared for *The Russian Review* as part of a symposium of comments on the seminal article by Edward Keenan, "Muscovite Political Folkways," *The Russian Review*, XLV:2 (April 1986). My contribution appeared as "Russian

Political Culture and the Post-Revolutionary Imp[ ]
1987; copyright © 1987 by *The Russian Review*).

The first two sections of Chapter 4, "The Intellig[ ]
of Reform: Khrushchev," are taken from an artic[ ]
the invitation of the Gramsci Institute's Bologna [ ]
number of the quarterly *Transizione* (February 19[ ]
current Soviet reforms. It appeared as "Il potere e l'ir[ ]
Power and the Intelligentsia; copyright © 1988 by[ ]   [ ]ne
balance of that article constitutes Chapter 6, "The Inte[ ] [ ]ntsia and the
Success of Reform: From Brezhnev to Gorbachev." The remainder of
Chapter 4 is based on a paper, "The Critical Intelligentsia and the Failure
of Khrushchev's Reform," that I was invited to prepare for the international
conference organized by the Feltrinelli Foundation and the Centro Studi
Paesi dell'Est of the Gramsci Foundation, "The XX Congress and Its
Aftermath," held in Florence, October 2–5, 1986. I am grateful to Fabio
Bettanin for reading the paper for me in my absence occasioned by
illness. The original text was published in the *Atti* (Proceedings) of the
conference (Milan: Feltrinelli Foundation, 1988; copyright © 1988 by
Fondazione Giacomo Feltrinelli).

Chapter 5, "The Political System and Generational Change," is an
outgrowth of a commentary that I delivered at a panel on "The Soviet
Political Leadership" at the Third World Congress of Slavists, Washington,
October 1985. Archie Brown, chair of that panel, undertook to edit a
book based on revised versions of the panel papers, which has been
published as *Political Leadership in the Soviet Union* (London: Macmillan,
1988; copyright © 1988 by The Macmillan Company). My contribution
was entitled "Political Processes and Generational Change."

The final chapter, "The Legacy of the Revolution," was written as
one of a series of comments on the essays by Zdeněk Mlynař, the Czech
reformer and Gorbachev's university roommate in the early 1950s,
published by *Rinascita*, the political weekly of the Italian Communist
Party, in the winter of 1986–1987. It appeared as "Il risveglio del
rivoluzionario russo" (The Revival of the Russian Revolutionary), *Rinascita*, February 14, 1987.

In all cases I am indebted to the editors or publishers of the journals
and collections concerned for their kind permission to use material
originally published by them in the present work.

In every instance I owe a debt of gratitude to the individuals who
originally invited me to undertake the articles incorporated in my
respective chapters: for Chapter 1, Professor Massimo L. Salvadori of
the University of Turin; for Chapter 2, Professor Herbert Ellison, former
Secretary of the Kennan Institute; for Chapter 3, Professor Daniel Field,
editor of *The Russian Review*; for Chapter 4, Dr. Federico Argentieri and

rgio Bertolissi of the Gramsci Institute; for Chapter 5, Professor
chie Brown of Oxford University; for Chapter 6, Professor Stefano
Bianchini of the University of Milan; and for Chapter 7, the late Romano
Ledda, editor of *Rinascita*.

Needless to say, the judgments I have arrived at in this work and
the idiosyncrasies they may represent are my own responsibility.

A couple of remarks on my approach: The reader will note that I
employ rather different methodologies—theoretical, empirical, or nar-
rative—in successive chapters. This choice has been governed by the
nature of the problem I take up in each case. The Italian audience to
whom the majority of these chapters was originally addressed is reflected
in my frequent selection of Italian sources for illustrations and comments,
but in any case these authors represent a significant body of expertise
on Soviet affairs of which English-speaking readers may appreciate being
made aware.

The bulk of the manuscript was originally typed by Mrs. Mabel Brown
and Mrs. Bridget Butler, while the difficult job of incorporating my
revisions was undertaken by my wife, Alice M. Daniels; I am deeply
appreciative to all. Susan McEachern of Westview Press was a constantly
helpful guide in editorial matters.

Robert V. Daniels

PART ONE

Barriers to Change

1

The Foundations of Stalinism

The natural baseline for judging change in the Soviet Union and the possibility of serious reform is the system of political power and economic and social institutions fashioned by Joseph Stalin during his twenty-five years of personal rule. To be sure, Stalinism in the full sense of the term came to an end in the year 1956, in a crisis of disbelief. When Nikita Khrushchev acknowledged the crimes of Stalin's purges and the fraudulence of Stalin's claims to genius, a quarter-century of self-righteous propaganda and doctrinal manipulation was wiped away. The international Communist movement and the Soviet Union itself had been conditioned all this time to regard Stalin's pronouncements and policies as the absolute in revolutionary virtue. De-Stalinization left them both without a clear sense of authority or direction.

For the movement outside the Soviet Union, including the ruling parties in Eastern Europe, Stalinism ceased to be a model for their politics, except insofar as the Russians could sustain it by force. Within the Soviet Union, the reaction was not allowed to go so far. While the "excesses" of the "cult of personality" were repudiated, the essential features of the Stalinist system—totalitarian government, command economics, political control of every form of organized social activity, and the manipulation of cultural values and historical truth—all persisted. These features remain in force in the Soviet Union, and they pose for the new leadership of Mikhail Gorbachev a fundamental challenge in the pursuit of reform and modernization.

The divergence between the Soviet Union and its foreign affiliates in their responses to de-Stalinization reflected the dual nature of Stalinism as a historical phenomenon. In one respect it was the terror of one man's egomanic despotism, symbolized by the Gulag. This was the side of Stalinism that Khrushchev rejected when he condemned Stalin's record beginning with the purges of the mid-1930s. But in another respect Stalinism was the reflection of problems and attitudes deeply rooted in the history of Russia, including its autocratic tradition, its economic and cultural backwardness, and its experience of violent revolution. This side of Stalinism, responsible for the consolidation of socialism, the modernization of the country, and the mobilization of formidable national power, became solidly institutionalized in the Soviet political and economic structure, and has therefore been far more difficult to change.

1. The Meaning of Stalinism

Stalinism by universal usage is a term of opprobrium, even of horror. The word itself was not used under Stalin, though "Stalinist" (*stalinskii*) appeared frequently in connection with his proclaimed triumphs. Reference to Stalin's historical record as "Stalinism" implies the critical rejection of his claim to represent the most progressive stage so far in the evolution of human society.

Agreement on the barbaric reality of Stalinism, now acknowledged by independent political observers of all persuasions, leads to more difficult questions. How could such a system arise in the course of a revolution that aimed to create the most just, democratic, and progressive society on earth? How could its leaders maintain these goals in words while in deeds perverting them beyond all imagination? How could they win the confidence of foreign revolutionaries and idealists, as they still do in various countries of the Third World?

The answers to these questions depend on a historical understanding of the sources of Stalinism, yet here is where critical authorities differ most among themselves. Was Stalinism merely the manifestation of a single aberrant personality, or was it the necessary outcome of the long-term processes of Russia's history? Was it a development unique to Russia, or just one particular example of the twentieth-century phenomenon of totalitarianism?

The definition of Stalinism has a direct bearing on how one understands the legacy of that era and the possibility of overcoming it. If the system of Stalinism were essentially the creature of its namesake, his demise should have opened the door for fundamental changes in the Soviet Union. But nothing happened there in the course of de-Stalinization on the order of the unsettling occurrences in Eastern Europe and the international Communist movement. For Russia, Stalinism was not merely the aberration of one despotic individual, it was embedded in the total historical situation. To the extent that the Stalin legacy stemmed from the whims and obsessions of a paranoid dictator, to that extent it was readily reformable. But to the extent that it represented an institutionalized response to difficult Russian problems, including the incomplete industrial transformation, the shock dealt by revolution to traditional expectations about authority, and the menace of foreign enemies, it resisted essential modification.

Stalinism may be summarized as a synthesis of certain powerful historical influences, both Russian and universal, accomplished by a unique individual who was able to add his personal stamp to the amalgam. Stalin built on the experience of modernization and the world-wide attraction of socialism, as well as the unfolding process of revolution which these stimuli engendered. He melded these universals of the modern world with the oldest authoritarian and nationalistic urges of Russian political culture, and with the challenge of survival in a hostile international environment. Finally, he brought all these elements together under the aegis of one of the cruelest and farthest-reaching despotisms known to history. Such was Stalinism: the compound of socialism, industrialism, revolution, nationalism, bureaucratic hierarchy and unlimited terror.

The nature of Stalinism as a product of these historical forces as well as of the power-lust of its leader defined both the crisis of Stalinism and the possibilities of an alternative. De-Stalinization as Khrushchev practiced it addressed the personal component in Stalinism—the terror, the xenophobia, the insane claim to omniscience and omnipotence. It could not, nor did it try, to undo Stalinism as the product of Russia's past. This could only be addressed by foreign sympathizers with the Russian Revolution and the Soviet experiment in socialism who, unburdened by the Russian milieu that had generated the elements of Stalinism, were able to call into question the bases of that system as well as its superstructure of political caprice and terror.

2. Stalinism and Marxism

Stalin always insisted, as have his successors up to now, that the system he built was the realization of the socialist society predicted and urged by Marx and Engels. This assertion has gone uncontested not only by the Stalinist Left but by most commentators on the Right, who gladly cite the horrors of Stalinism as proof of the perniciousness of Marxist doctrine or even of socialism in general.

The rejection of Stalinism by the Left outside of Russia was long delayed by their ideological commitment to Marxism. As long as they believed that Stalin's regime in Russia represented the realization of Marx's scientific socialism, it was natural for those in the camp of social justice and class equality to overlook the deformations attributable to unfortunate Russian circumstances, and stand together in solidarity with the first socialist country on the face of the globe. This reasoning, of course, was vital to Stalin in his efforts to rally foreign sympathizers to the defense of the interests of the Soviet Union. It underscored the importance for Stalin and for his successors of maintaining the ideological facade of Marxism to attract foreign support.

Stalinism's obvious divergence from the expectations of Marxism, above all in its perpetuation of the bureaucratic hierarchy and the totalitarian state, suggests that there are major limitations in the Marxian theory of history. In its original form, Marxism fails to account for the possibility of socialist revolution in a relatively backward country such as Russia. It fails to consider the impact of unmet developmental and defense needs on a premature socialist regime. It rests on a questionable faith in the self-governing potential of the proletariat, especially dubious in a semi-developed country, and (apart from certain warnings about the influence of the old state bureaucracy) fails to recognize the modern postcapitalist trend everywhere toward the exercise of power independently of property ownership by state or corporate managers.

There remains another theory of Marxism's evil ideological influence that has come into vogue in recent years. This is the argument advanced by the American Catholic political philosopher Eric Voegelin, among others, that the commitment of Marxists to a political belief at one and the same time both deterministic and utopian was a form of "gnosticism," a heresy of hubris, leading them inexorably to the monumental crimes of Stalinism.[1] In this view, the Marxian vision dictated the Stalinist outcome not because the communist utopia was inevitable but because it was impossible.

The problem with this reasoning is that it substitutes for Marx's economic determinism a sort of philosophical determinism, asserted after the fact, holding that the Marxist ideas championed by the Russian revolutionaries, though wrong, were wholly or mainly responsible for the Stalinist outcome of their efforts. Some conservative thinkers like J. L. Talmon connect the Stalinist horror, i.e., "totalitarian democracy," back to the whole tradition of rationalistic social change ever since the Enlightenment.[2] But philosophical determinism is unrealistic in presuming that people are driven more by the logic of their beliefs than by their underlying values or by the facts of their situation. It fails to account for those Marxists, the Social Democrats, who rejected the use of revolutionary force. It neglects the powerful historical circumstances which have conditioned the efforts of Marxist revolutionaries, starting with Russia. It underestimates the individual psychological proclivities that may draw fanatical adherents of a given doctrine (one could cite Christianity as well as Marxism) into forms of behavior highly antithetical to the original spirit of their belief.

When the full record is considered, it makes little sense to try to understand Stalinism either as the victorious implementation of Marxism or as the pure fury of fanatics who cannot achieve their imagined goal. Ideologically, Stalinism meant the abandonment of the Marxian program and the pragmatic acceptance of postrevolutionary Russian reality, while the power of the dictatorship was used to reinterpret and enforce Marxist doctrine as a tool of propaganda and legitimation. No genuine ideological imperative remained. Marxism could be made to appear to justify Stalinism, but it was no longer allowed to serve either as a policy directive or an explanation of reality. To extend Marx's own formulation, Marxism under Stalin became the ideological "false consciousness" of New Class rule.

3. Stalinism and the Revolution

Stalinism was not generated by ideology, but by actual historical events. Apart from the experience of revolution Stalinism could not have existed. Neither the nature nor the achievements of Stalinism can be understood without placing the phenomenon properly within its historical context in revolutionary Russia.

For an interpretation of history that puts revolution at its center, Marxism is oddly deficient in its theory of revolution. As the Russian experience so clearly shows, revolution is no simple matter of the class struggle of the bourgeoisie against the feudal nobility and then of the proletariat against the capitalists. It involves a mix of volatile social elements—in Russia, intellectuals as well as proletarians and peasants—reflecting the stage of development the country has reached when the crisis erupts. Russian Marxists have always had to struggle with the fusion of two theoretical stages of revolution into one actual upheaval.

Secondly, Marxism fails to recognize that revolution is not a simple, momentary event. As the Emperor Napoleon said in exile, "A revolution cannot be made; neither can it be stopped."[3] Revolution in the fullest sense of the word is not an event but a process, not a simple overturn or a mere coup but a long struggle over the breakdown and rebuilding of a nation's basic institutions. It is a crisis of development, rooted in a nation's history and its experience of modernization.

Revolution is not a mere political tactic that can be invoked at will by revolutionaries, nor can it, as Friedrich Engels observed, be steered precisely to the goal that revolutionaries may have in mind.[4] Revolutions typically swing from beneficent reformism toward violence and fanaticism, and then to opportunistic consolidation and reconstituted authoritarianism. Ultimately they betray most of the hopes that animated their original adherents.

The political structure of Stalinism had its origins in the early era of revolutionary extremism, the time of the Russian Civil War and War

Communism. Under the influence of Lenin's philosophy of "democratic centralism," one-party power, and the struggle for survival against the armies of the counterrevolution and Allied intervention, the Communist Party acquired a form and a spirit essentially military in nature. Robert C. Tucker refers to the "culture of War Communism" as the psychological source of the militance and authoritarianism that attracted the party bureaucracy to Stalin in the course of the 1920s.[5] While the revolution was in a period of remission during the years of the New Economic Policy, Stalin developed his own power base in the party apparatus, perfecting the *nomenklatura* system of appointments and ranks, and eventually establishing personal control over the Central Committee and the Politburo. By the late 1920s, controlling the only effective organ of power, Stalin was in a position comparable to that enjoyed by Napoleon Bonaparte with his command of the French army, to realize the potential for personal despotism offered by the postrevolutionary condition of his country.

This final phase defines the relationship of Stalinism to the revolution. Stalinism took shape as the specific Russian instance of the postrevolutionary dictatorship, with all that this implied in the rebuilding of coercive authority, the synthesis of revolutionary rhetoric with traditional nationalistic and authoritarian emotions, and the mobilization of new national energy. Where Bonaparte immediately went on the offensive against the rest of Europe, Stalin attacked his own people, to coerce them through collectivization and forced industrialization into building the economic basis of new national power. The purges that followed in the mid-thirties defy comparison with any revolutionary precedent, certainly not with Robespierre's terror in the first flush of revolutionary fanaticism. When viewed along with Stalin's simultaneous condemnation of modernistic culture, libertarian and egalitarian social thought, and antinational history, the era of the purges can be seen as a *de facto* counterrevolution, perhaps the functional equivalent of an imperial Restoration in the Russian revolutionary process.

In the perspective of the revolutionary process, the debate about Marx's responsibility for Lenin and Lenin's responsibility for Stalin loses much of its meaning. As the terminal phase of revolution in Russia, Stalinism quite naturally contradicted Marx's predictions and violated his prescriptions. Thanks to the nominal perpetuation of the Communist Party and its Marxist dogma, Stalinism fulfilled the role of a counterrevolution in revolutionary garb.

Although he adapted himself adroitly to the waning phases of the revolution, Stalin was not free of personal responsibility for the ultimate shape of postrevolutionary Russia. A postrevolutionary dictator, taking advantage of a battered nation's need for authority, enjoys great scope to impose his personal idiosyncrasies. Like other upstart leaders at this point in the process, Stalin was an egomanic opportunist. He was evidently driven to compensate for his own inadequacies and perceived humiliations by murdering all his past rivals, rewriting history, identifying himself with the power and prestige of the Russian nation ("the Great-Russian chauvinism of Russified non-Russians," as Lenin termed it[6]), glorifying himself as the coryphaeus of all knowledge, and turning the country's intellectual life into a pathetic parody.

As noted already, Stalin's actions as a postrevolutionary dictator had two different sides. One was naturally called for by the point that Russia had reached in its revolutionary process and in its efforts at modernization. The other was the expression of purely personal whim and tyranny by an individual whom George Kennan has termed "a man of incredible criminality, of a criminality effectively without limits."[7] These two aspects of Stalinism were implicitly distinguished by Khrushchev when he fixed on the year 1934 to limit his retrospective de-Stalinization of the historical record.

4. Stalinism and Modernization

The most indisputable achievement of Stalinism, the success that compelled Khrushchev to accept the cost of the excesses committed by Stalin up to 1934, was to set in motion the machinery of state-planned industrialization. Armed with the powers of the totalitarian state and the command economy, Stalin was able to channel Russia's resources into the extraordinary tempo of industrial construction that the country pursued during the first two Five-Year Plans. He thus laid the economic base whereby the Soviet Union was able to withstand the German onslaught of World War II and then to challenge the United States in military competition in the era of the Cold War.

Stalin's industrialization drive was anticipated by the Left Opposition of the 1920s led by Trotsky and his economic spokesman Preobrazhensky, though they had little idea of the degree of coercion that Stalin would impose in the pursuit of the goal of modernization. They were trying to address Russia's incomplete modernization that still had to be confronted after the premature victory of a socialist revolution. In turn, Stalin's mobilization of a violent new national effort after the respite of the NEP reflected the characteristic tendency of a postrevolutionary dictatorship to maximize its power by waging war, on its own people if not on its external neighbors.

The successes of Stalinism in industrialization were bought at tremendous cost, not only in economic terms and in immediate human suffering, but also in an enduring institutional deformation of Soviet society. The underpinning of Stalin's approach to modernization was anything but modern—it was, in essence, the reintroduction of serfdom. In this Stalin resembled Peter the Great, whose reforms in the name of Westernization rested on more coercion and unfreedom, not less. As the next chapter shows, Stalin militarized the whole organization of the Soviet economy. In industry this took the form of the command relationship between the center and the enterprise, and the discipline imposed on the workers when the trade unions were converted into another agency of pressure from above. In the rural sector, through the mechanism of the forcibly established collective farms and legal restrictions on freedom of movement, the Soviet peasantry was subjected to state command and control so that the authorities could appropriate the grain needed to feed the cities and the army and to pay for the import of equipment required by the industrialization drive. So relentless was the collective farm system that delivery quotas could be enforced even upon drought-stricken Ukrainian villagers, causing the artificial, unacknowledged famine of 1932–1933 and its casualties running into the millions.

The Stalinist method of industrialization was indeed one effective way of pursuing the goal of modernization and competitive national power, but it was not the only alternative. One may cite Japan, whose economic growth rate in the same era was comparable, or the program of development by means of the market socialism of the New Economic Policy, vainly defended by Bukharin. Indeed, recent studies of Stalin's hasty development program have suggested that long-term growth would actually have been higher, if the Soviet Union had followed Bukharin's gradualist program rather than Stalin's.[8]

Stalin's choice of a method of industrialization was not based on rational economic calculation or forethought. It was a political decision, arrived at during 1928–1929 when he was fighting the Right Opposition and looking for issues that would enable him to condemn Bukharin and his friends as deviators from the general line of the party. They in fact were only defending the cautious method of planning developed during the NEP. Stalin simply raised his targets for the tempo of industrialization and collectivization until the impossibility of the pace forced the Right Opposition to speak out, whereupon they were condemned and politically destroyed. The result of this episode was that Stalin became committed to the methods of command in both industry and agriculture. By an accident of politics he had stumbled upon a logical new alternative for Russia's development, though it was neither the most humane nor the most economical way to go.

Stalin's approach to modernization, formulated for narrowly political reasons, not on the basis either of abstract doctrine or economic pragmatism, was permanently institutionalized and bequeathed to his successors. Up to a point the Stalinist system of economics appeared to justify itself in its impressive record of industrial growth and technological achievement, not only in the 1930s but from World War II down to the early 1970s. In economics, the crisis of Stalinism came not in 1956 but a quarter-century later, when the growth rate fell to a crawl, the technology gap vis-à-vis the capitalist powers widened, and the frustrated expectations of Soviet consumers contributed to rising social pathology and ebbing national morale. Stalinist economics was a workable alternative for the early and middle phases of industrialization; it became counterproductive in addressing the new economic challenges of recent decades. Soviet Russia awaits an economic de-Stalinization under Gorbachev comparable to the political and cultural de-Stalinization it was accorded under Khrushchev.

5. Stalinism and Totalitarianism

In most critical commentary, particularly in the English-speaking countries, Stalinism is still subsumed in the concept of totalitarianism. There is some confusion in academic ranks over the term, and a tendency to restrict the "totalitarian model" to the period prior to the repudiation of Stalin's personal excesses. This is an error. If totalitarianism has any generic meaning at all, it still applies to the Soviet Union today despite the functional divisions and putative "interest groups" that exist within the system.

In the great volume of literature on the theme, totalitarianism has been accurately described but poorly explained. For example, Carl J. Friedrich and Zbigniew Brzezinski analyzed all the features common to Fascist, Nazi, and Communist regimes but could only explain their origins on the basis of simple ideological fanaticism.[9] The totalitarian model generally lacks a sense of the historical situations and forces that make totalitarian regimes possible, above all the context of revolution.

Totalitarianism of the Left—Stalinism—is a direct and natural product of revolution. Totalitarianism of the Right is the outcome of a counter-revolutionary struggle against an actual or possible revolution. In either case, every available means of coercion, amplified by modern technology in weapons, surveillance, and record-keeping, is employed to preserve power and control society. Totalitarianism is the characteristic twentieth-century form of the post-revolutionary dictatorship, whether it has been arrived at from the Right or from the Left.

There is much truth in the notion that in totalitarianism "the extremes meet." As the Right becomes more revolutionary and the Left becomes more traditionalist, differences between the two totalitarianisms shrink to matters of degree and rhetoric. Only the leftist language of Stalinism obscured the extent to which it psychologically approached the more openly acknowledged authoritarian principles of the Right. The party, conceived by Lenin as an instrument of revolution, was transformed during the 1920s into a permanent means of autocratic rule, through the bureaucratic structure of the party apparatus, charged with surveillance and control over every aspect of society. Ever since the factional struggle against the Left Opposition, the mentality of the *apparatchiki* has been distinguished by a fierce insistence on unity, unanimity, and conformity to the will of the leader. Stalinism evidences the same authoritarian personality that has been described by Erich Fromm and Theodor Adorno in the Fascist and Nazi regimes.[10] Through the party's elaborate system of cadre selection and training these traits have been perpetuated in the Soviet power structure. In Stalin's later years, distinctly rightist elements of ideology were overtly or covertly embraced. These notably included Great-Russian nationalism and anti-Semitism, and today these sentiments are the main popular sources of whatever genuine political enthusiasm the regime enjoys.

In its thoroughness of control, above all in economic life, Stalinist totalitarianism went well beyond its counterparts of the Right. Russian traditions of centralism and subservience helped make this extreme possible, while the needs of industrialization and defense gave it a purpose. Totalitarianism was not fully realized in Russia until Stalin applied the power of the party to collectivize the peasants, militarize the urban economy, and tyrannize all sectors of cultural and intellectual life. The terror that followed far transcended any violence inflicted by the totalitarians of the Right upon their own nationals, and equalled in scope and irrationality Hitler's campaigns of international genocide.

6. Stalinism and Socialism

Throughout the worst of the terror and privation inflicted by his regime, Stalin was able to soften or deflect the judgments of reality by claiming to have achieved the goal of socialism. In many minds Stalinism gained indisputable legitimation by its attachment to the century-old sentiments of social justice that the term socialism implied for the Left, the labor movement, and anti-imperialists in most countries. In the official Stalinist view Soviet Russia was the first socialist society in the world, the beacon light that all other nations had to follow.

What merit is there in the Soviet claim to represent not only a form of socialism but its highest attainment? The contention that Soviet Russia must be socialist, because it is the embodiment of the proletarian revolution, is a myth vigorously disputed by the non-Communist or anti-Stalinist Left. Since 1956 no one outside the reach of Moscow's ideological discipline has defended the claim that Russia has laid down the one true road to socialism. Many anti-Stalinists have gone on to maintain that the Soviet Union is not socialist at all, but rather a form of "etatism," as the Yugoslavs say, or "bureaucratic state capitalism," or "totalitarian state economy," as Rudolf Hilferding once described it.[11]

These formulations are understandable as efforts to deny the Soviets the political legitimacy that the label "socialist" might convey, but they depend on unconvincing exercises in semantic hair-splitting. If socialism is to be given any simple and workable definition, it is the principle of social control over economic activity, however organized and under whatever political system. The Soviet system may be repugnant on political or ethical grounds, but it is nonetheless a system of socialism based on social control—in fact, extreme and uncompromising social control—over economic activity. The perfection of a nearly total system of socialized economy was a distinct accomplishment of Stalinism. To this day legislation promulgated when the NEP was liquidated is still in force, to suppress all private enterprise (save the private plots and family operations), and to impose criminal sanctions against any private trade as "speculation" and against any private employment as "exploitation."

If Marxian dogma is disregarded, the actuality of socialism under Stalinism can be recognized without conceding that it was the only genuine or possible version of socialism, good or bad. Stalinism was only one of many alternative forms of socialist society. To be sure, it was a form quite unexpected by any of the theoretical progenitors of the ideal, transformed and deformed as it was by Russian conditions of economic backwardness, autocratic tradition, and revolutionary violence.

Stalin's traumatic modernization program of the 1930s was always officially described as "building socialism." In effect, the attainment of the Marxian state of grace was equated with the expansion of industrial production. According to Stalin the stage of "socialism," or what Marx termed the "first stage of communism," was reached when he promulgated the 1936 constitution, because the exploiter classes had been liquidated. Since that time Soviet theorists have devised various ritualistic categories to describe the country's progress—"perfecting socialism" or "preparing the foundations for the transition to communism." Presently, the system describes itself as "developed socialism" or "real existing socialism." All of these formulations serve to postpone the question of proceeding with the implementation of Marx's higher stage of "communism"—a utopia which neither Stalin nor his successors have had any intention of implementing.

Granted that Stalinism succeeded in implanting an extreme form of socialism (though not in transforming human nature according to the collectivist ideal of the "New Soviet Man"), how successfully did the socialist system function? In the rapid advance of heavy industry and military potential Stalinist socialism was a distinct success, though it has now reached the point of diminishing returns. In other respects, in agriculture and in the petty economy of trade, crafts and consumer services, Stalinist socialism came near to disaster, and its retrogressive effect has still not been overcome. By collectivizing agriculture and nationalizing petty-proprietor enterprise, Stalin made the choice not to wait for capitalism or even market socialism to accomplish the process of "primary capital accumulation" in what could have been an economically more progressive way. In respect both to industrial construction and the socialization of small enterprise, Stalinist socialism was not the sequel to capitalism but an alternative to it, supplanting the capitalist mode of concentrating a country's resources for development, and using the coercive powers of the state to this end. Stalinism involved a fundamental reorientation in the goals as well as the methods of socialism, abandoning the traditional socialist pursuit of justice in the distribution of economic values in favor of economic mobilization to maximize production, primarily in the interest of the state and its military power.

The Russian experience shows that there is no historic inevitability to the perfect socialism that idealists of the Left have envisaged. Betraying even Russia's own spirit of absolute democratization that had erupted in 1917, Stalinism fashioned a system of bureaucratic state socialism, paralleling the latest capitalist trends of organizational concentration, enforced by the political mechanisms of totalitarianism, and guided by the imperatives of modernization and national power. Perhaps all this was hard to avoid, given the burden of Russia's historical legacy and the requirements of successful competition and even survival in the modern world. But for the cause of social justice around the globe, it was a tragedy that Russia, of all places, should be the locale of the world's first great socialist experiment.

7. Stalinism and the World

Stalinism was a paradox of revolutionary theory and counterrevolutionary reality, not only in its internal nature but also in its international conduct. While trumpeting the revolutionary language of proletarian internationalism, Stalinism actually effected a profound turn away from the outside world. The direction of the shift was temporarily masked by Stalin's pursuit of conventional diplomacy and alliances from the beginning of the Popular Front era to the end of World War II. But this was the same time when he was reviving Russian nationalism, cultivating an espionage mania to excuse his purges, and denouncing every sort of foreign influence. Building formidable foundations for Russian imperial power, Stalinism set Russia against the world, not only against the capitalist world but against the revolutionary world insofar as it was not Soviet-controlled. Soviet Russia reverted to the xenophobia rooted in the oldest layers of Russian political culture that had come to the surface with the Stalinist leadership.

The core of Stalinist foreign policy was and remains nothing more nor less than the maximization of the security and influence of the Soviet state. Marxist doctrine, though dogmatically asserted as the legitimation of each step taken by the Soviet Union in its foreign relations, lost all guiding force, just as it had in the country's internal affairs. Through his agencies of indoctrination internally and through the Comintern externally, Stalin was able to redefine Marxist goals and categories so flexibly that entire social systems could be reclassified from reactionary to progressive or vice versa depending on whether their governments happened to be allies or adversaries of the Soviet Union. Even a Communist country, as in the case of Yugoslavia, could be transformed from socialism into fascism by a stroke of Stalin's pen. It is obvious that for Stalin, in foreign relations as well as in internal politics, anyone beyond the reach of his army and police was a potential enemy. Foreign Communist refugees, even including the leader of Hungary's 1919 revolution, Bela Kun, learned this to their sorrow in the purges of the 1930s, as did a long series of National Communist leaders soon after they had been installed in power in Eastern Europe in the late 1940s.

If Stalin had one positive principle in his foreign policy, it was Russian nationalism, buttressed as occasion demanded with Marxist-Leninist language. During the test that Stalinism underwent in World War II, Russian nationalism was the main propaganda theme. Marxism-Leninism, revived after the war, was fused with Russian nationalism, to become essentially an ideology of super-power confrontation between the "socialist" and "imperialist" camps. This was the atmosphere in which Stalin sealed the country off from foreign contacts of every sort, strangely so for a regime that claimed to be the world model for the future. Far from any international revolutionary confidence, it was fear of contamination and exposure that governed Stalin's political view of the outside world.

One of the most remarkable achievements of Stalinism was its transformation of an international revolutionary movement into an instrument to serve the interests of the Soviet Union. This was only made possible by the imposition of Stalinist-type control by Moscow over the affairs of the foreign Communist parties, including leadership selection, political tactics, and ideological acknowledgment of Soviet guidance. The demand for such conformity originated with Lenin's Twenty-One Conditions of 1920, but it did not become a reality until the "Bolshevization" of the Communist International in the middle and later 1920s. Attacking first the supporters of the ultra-Left in Russia, then the supporters of Trotsky, then the supporters of Bukharin, Stalin succeeded by 1930 in expelling from the movement practically all the original founders of the various Communist parties. Thereafter, with the notable exception of China, the Comintern parties proved by and large to be dependable defenders both of Soviet ideological claims and of the zig-zag line of Soviet foreign policy, from the "United Front" and the eclectic search for allies in the 1920s, to the "Third Period" of renewed revolutionary rhetoric from 1928 to 1934, to the Popular Front and Collective Security, and on to the period of the pact with Hitler and the Great Patriotic War. This was going on, ironically, while Stalin was transforming the Soviet Union internally into a conservative totalitarianism and burying the last embers of true revolutionary feeling in his counterrevolutionary purges.

From the standpoint of Russian national aspirations, international Stalinism was extraordinarily successful during the years immediately following the end of the war. Russian power filled the vacuum left in Eastern Europe by the collapse of Nazi Germany, and thereby brought into the Soviet sphere practically all the lands eyed by the Pan-Slavists of the nineteenth century as targets for Russian domination. Not only this—Stalin was able to impose on his new East European satellites the model of totalitarian socialism that had taken shape in Russia under his direction. This was an unnatural achievement, not only because it represented a coercive foreign imposition on the national life of Eastern Europe, but also because the totalitarian intensity of the Stalinist model reflected specifically Russian conditions of autocracy, backwardness, and revolution. Once the grip of Stalinism was relaxed by Khrushchev, it was natural if not inevitable that the reaction against it would be much sharper in Eastern Europe, particularly in those more developed and more sophisticated countries better described as Central European.

In a broader context, Stalin's program in Eastern Europe was just a part of the mission that he took on to counterbalance the United States in the postwar confrontation between the two superpowers. His success was considerable but not unqualified. Stalin signally failed in his effort to use Western Communists to prevent the solidification of the NATO alliance against him, and he was unable to keep the major part of Germany out of the Western alignment. Because of his guiding Cold War premise of the inherent hostility of the outside world, he could not see that his own counterproductive tactics of political and military pressure were responsible for much of the actual animosity that he encountered. The same premise explains his short-sighted failure to exploit the nationalism of colonial or newly independent nations, as his successors have so effectively done.

Stalinism, a Russian development intimately tied to Russian national interests, proved itself to be inapplicable anywhere else in the world except by the exertion of Russian power. Other countries and parties in the Communist movement were kept loyal to Stalinism only by various combinations of deception and force. When the magic spell was broken by Khrushchev, they were ready to go as far as their political circumstances permitted to challenge the Stalinist model and to reject Soviet dictation of their respective destinies.

8. The Limits of Stalinism

In its most extreme form Stalinism proved too severe even for the country that had engendered it. The excrescences of terror, cultural repression, and xenophobia that stemmed primarily from Stalin's personal idiosyncrasies—not to say madness—did not survive his death. On the other hand, the structural aspects of Stalinism, reflecting the historic experiences and needs of postrevolutionary Russia, proved impervious to serious reform for another generation. These included, obviously, the entire economic structure of planned industry and collectivized agriculture, the apparatus of political control, and the social system of bureaucratic hierarchy with its cadres advancing through the ranks of the nomenklatura to share at one level or another in the exercise of power.

The reforms of Khrushchev were hailed all over the world as de-Stalinization. Within the Soviet Union, by ameliorating the most destructive and demoralizing excesses of Stalinism, reform actually made the basic Stalinist system more tolerable and more durable. Outside the Soviet Union the effects of de-Stalinization were far more serious. At the signal of Khrushchev's Secret Speech, the mental hold of Stalinism both in the East European governments and in the Western Communist parties gave way, with spectacular consequences. Without the rigor of Stalin's own Stalinism, both in its ideological claims and in its readiness to use coercion, Moscow could no longer maintain the political dominance over the international movement that it had enjoyed for a generation. 1956 was not only the year of the crisis of Stalinism, but the year of its end as a meaningful political phenomenon beyond the tips of the Soviet Army's bayonets.

Notes

1. See, e.g., Eric Voegelin, *Science, Politics and Gnosticism* (Chicago: Regnery, 1968).

2. J. L. Talmon, *The Rise of Totalitarian Democracy* (Boston: Beacon Press, 1951).

3. J. Christopher Herold, ed., *The Mind of Napoleon: A Selection from His Written and Spoken Words* (New York: Columbia University Press, 1955), p. 64.

4. Engels to Vera Zasulich, April 22, 1885, Karl Marx and Friedrich Engels, *Selected Correspondence, 1846–1895* (New York: International Publishers, 1947), pp. 437–438.

5. Robert C. Tucker, "Stalinism as Revolution from Above," in Tucker, *Stalinism: Essays in Historical Interpretation* (New York: Norton, 1977), pp. 91–94.

6. V. I. Lenin, "Continuation of Notes, December 30–31, 1922," in Richard Pipes, *The Formation of the Soviet Union: Communism and Nationalism, 1917–1923* (Cambridge, Mass.: Harvard University Press, 1954), pp. 273–277; Soviet edition, Lenin, *Pis'mo syezdu* (Letter to the Congress, Moscow: Gospolitizdat, 1956).

7. George F. Kennan, *Russia and the West under Lenin and Stalin* (Boston: Little, Brown, 1961), p. 254.

8. See, e.g., Holland Hunter, "The Overambitious First Soviet Five-Year Plan," *The Slavic Review*, XXXII:2 (June 1973).

9. Carl J. Friedrich and Zbigniew Brzezinski, *Totalitarian Government and Autocracy* (Cambridge, Mass.: Harvard University Press, 1956).

10. Erich Fromm, *Escape from Freedom* (New York: Farrar and Rinehart, 1941); Theodor Adorno et al., *The Authoritarian Personality* (New York: Harper, 1950).

11. Rudolf Hilferding, "State Capitalism or Totalitarian State Economy," *Modern Review*, LXXXI:6 (June 1947).

2

Lenin, Stalin, and the
Military Model of Socialism

The nature of Stalinism and the question of the socialist character of the Soviet system have remained subjects of profound disagreement outside the Soviet Union ever since de-Stalinization had its impact in the 1950s. Vigorous debate has gone on both in Western academic quarters and among non-Soviet Marxists, in and out of power, over these basic issues. Are socialism and Stalinism inseparable or mutually exclusive? Can the Soviet system achieve reform only by abandoning socialism, or can it only achieve socialism by fundamentally reforming itself?

Anti-Stalin Marxists are attracted to the easy explanation that Stalinism represents the abandonment of genuine socialism. For example, three Hungarian dissident writers argue in *Dictatorship Over Needs* that Soviet society is neither capitalist nor socialist, nor even a transitional form, but a unique system based on class rule by a bureaucracy.[1] Official Yugoslav political theory describes the Soviet system not as socialism, but as "etatism."[2] "Socialism is *totally* incompatible with Stalinism, as it is with the totalitarian state and any other system of political oppression," writes the Yugoslav economist Branko Horvat.[3] Chinese thinking under Mao put down the Soviet model as the "capitalist road," and more recently China has attributed Soviet behavior to the expansionist interests of the bureaucratic class.[4] Adriano Guerra, a leading Italian Communist observer of the Soviet scene, recently said, "What has now faded away is the idea that the problems of the world can find their solution by following the example and the model of the Soviet Union and by identifying the struggle for world socialism with the policies of the Soviet state."[5] Notwithstanding such assertions, conservative thought in the West has long held that experiments in socialism lead inexorably toward totalitarianism of the Soviet type.[6]

While these arguments certainly dramatize the question whether the Soviet Union is socialist or not, none of them fully clarifies the issue.

Scholastic debates over what is and what is not socialism cannot take the place of accurate definition and a readiness to describe the Soviet system. It is more fruitful to ask what type and degree of socialism has developed in the course of the Soviet experience and what historical circumstances might be invoked to explain its development.

The term socialism is employed here as neutrally as possible, to mean any idea or practice of public control over economic enterprise. This definition is designedly loose, like the one given by the great French sociologist Emile Durkheim: "We denote as socialism every doctrine which demands the connection of all economic functions, or of certain among them . . . to the directing and conscious centers of society."[7]

Socialism as thus understood may come in various forms and degrees— total or partial, sudden or gradual, violent or peaceful, dictatorial or democratic. It is usually associated with state property and the nationalization of business, though this is not essential to the concept. Alternatives might include municipal enterprises, cooperative and communal organizations, worker participation in management, or forms of public planning and regulation that vitiate the nominal power of private ownership.

Historically, socialism is a heavily value-laden term—either positive or negative—and this makes its use risky in an analytic sense. Nonetheless, its prominence in world-wide political thought during the last 150 years makes it impossible to avoid. Fruitless debates occasioned by the unexamined use of the term are best set aside by addressing semantic issues at the outset.

To my mind, the Soviet Union represents a form of socialism, but a form governed by Russia's particular historical traditions, its revolutionary experience, and the currents of social evolution that it has shared with the rest of the modern or modernizing world. Much less can Soviet socialism be explained by the specific ideology of Marxism with which it is officially associated. But foreign reactions, whether favorable or antagonistic, have tended to be based on ideological superficialities. Either the Soviet Union is endorsed because it appears to be socialist, or socialism is rejected because it appears to be Soviet.

1. Lenin and the Military Model

If one observes the Soviet political, economic, and social system as it has developed over the past fifty or sixty years, with a blind eye to ideological labels, its basic military character is obvious. This applies both to its structure and to its spirit and purposes. To review the essential features of Stalinist totalitarianism—its centralized command structure, its ranks and hierarchies, the manner in which it mobilized resources,

the discipline in thought and action enforced by police and censorship apparatuses, and the solidarity of the nation in facing its external enemies—is to recite the normal characteristics of a military organization. Soviet Russia became a garrison state where everyone, in effect, was in the army. The French ex-Marxist critic Cornelius Castoriadis has termed it a "stratocracy," that is, a system ruled by military interests.[8] It is close to what the Marquis de Mirabeau (and perhaps Voltaire before him) said of Frederick the Great's Prussia: it is "not a country that has an army; it is an army that has a country."[9]

Such an outcome for a system dedicated to socialism is the ultimate paradox, considering that socialism until 1914 was identified everywhere with anti-militarist, anti-imperialist, anti-nationalist, and anti-authoritarian views. In the Soviet experience, socialism was turned from the antithesis of militarism into an instrument of militarism. It was used as a method of economic organization whereby the resources of society were maximally geared to serving the needs and priorities of the military interest. This transformation in the shape and purpose of Soviet socialism reflected diverse formative historical forces—the revolution, dogmatic Marxist-Leninist ideology, Russian backwardness and tradition, external threats, and the overall bureaucratic direction of modern society's evolution. But there was also a distinct history of choices and experiences under the Communist regime that must be taken into account to understand the militarized system that finally prevailed in Russia.

The militarization of socialism in Russia clearly had its beginning with Lenin. A military model of political organization and action was the core of Bolshevism as Lenin formulated it in his early writings and pursued it through his split with the Mensheviks. The Bolsheviks, in his view, should be "a regular army of tested fighters" stressing "organized preparation for battle."[10]

The writings of Marx and Engels, to be sure, bequeathed a certain psychological climate of combat inherent in the philosophy of class struggle. Engels went so far as to call Social Democratic voters "the international proletarian army."[11] But for Marx and Engels, the military model did not carry over into the organization of the future socialist society. Indeed, pointing to the outcome of the French Revolution of 1848 in military dictatorship, they were at pains to warn the working class against the danger of a bureaucratic power beyond its control.[12] They rarely if ever went so far as to use the term "class war"—a Soviet term that does not appear to have come into general use until the Russian Civil War made it a reality.

Lenin's entrancement with military modes of thinking applied not only to his conception of revolutionary political organization, but to the methods required for political success, both internally and internationally.

The experience of the 1905 revolution brought him to the view suggestive of Bismarck: "Major questions in the life of nations are settled only by force."[13] Hoping to follow up this first abortive assault on tsarism, he wrote, "We would be deceiving both ourselves and the people if we concealed from them the fact that the impending revolutionary action must take the form of a desperate, bloody war of extermination."[14] When international war broke out in 1914, it was not enough for Lenin to oppose the war effort as did left-wing socialists all over Europe. He denounced "priestly-sentimental and stupid sighing" about "peace no matter what," and called instead for "the transformation of the present imperialist war into a civil war."[15]

Lenin had a habit of getting very excited over new ideas that he liked or disliked, and immediately wove them into his Marxist world-view without stopping to think that Marxism was any less immutable. Thus it was regarding his infatuation with the classic Prussian strategist von Clausewitz, whom he discovered and read in Switzerland in 1915. What he extracted from Clausewitz was little more than the familiar maxim, "War is the pursuit of politics by other means," which he thereafter quoted at every opportunity.[16] This formula seemed to support his implicit conviction that politics had to be pursued by the most warlike means.

The thinness of Lenin's military study has not prevented present-day Soviet theorists from describing him as the fountainhead of Soviet military thought. According to the 1972 treatise by A. S. Milovidov and V. G. Kozlov, *The Philosophical Heritage of V. I. Lenin and Problems of Contemporary War,* "The brilliant theorist and architect of the new socialist world, V. I. Lenin, was also the most profound theorist in philosophical problems of modern war, armed forces and military science. With his name are associated the founding of the Soviet Armed Forces and their heroic history. . . . V. I. Lenin was the founder of Soviet military science."[17] Of course, it would be too much to expect Trotsky, who knew military matters from his experience as a correspondent during the Balkan Wars, to receive credit as the organizer of the Red Army. As for Trotsky's own view of Marxist military thought, he cautioned in a lecture in 1922 when he was still Commissar of War, "Even if one grants that 'military science' is a *science,* it is nevertheless impossible to grant that it can be built with the methods of Marxism; because historical materialism isn't at all a universal method for all sciences. . . . It is the greatest misconception to try to build in the special field of military matters by means of Marxism."[18] This is probably the best commentary that can be offered on the scientific level of official Soviet military philosophizing.

The fact remains that a military spirit, however sophomoric, marked Lenin's entire political career. Military modes of thought exude from almost everything he wrote. His vocabulary was replete with military metaphors—war, mobilization, offensive, strategy, and tactics. Force, arms, iron discipline, and the militant vanguard were always his ingredients for victory.

2. The Impact of Revolutionary Violence

It is ironic that the open political atmosphere of 1917 and the spontaneous surge of popular support for the Bolsheviks brought the party at the moment of its revolutionary victory to the most unmilitary point in its organizational history. So strong was the tide of ultra-democratic revolution that most of the Bolshevik leadership preferred to avoid a violent test of strength against the Provisional Government in the fall of 1917, and to wait for the Second Congress of Soviets to vote them into power. Lenin, by contrast, was obsessed with the opportunity of employing sympathetic army units and naval crews to effect a military coup against Kerensky's government. In the directives he sent to party headquarters from his hiding-place, he fulminated against the idea of delay. "History has made the *military* question now the fundamental *political* question."[19] A simple military action would decide the day. "We can seize *at once* the Winter Palace, the General Staff building, the telephone exchange, and all the largest printing establishments. . . . Kerensky will be compelled to *surrender*."[20] Lenin was not bothered by the logical contradiction between his conviction of the decisiveness of military action and the philosophy of historical materialism. As military thinkers must be, Lenin in his implicit philosophy was not determinist but voluntarist. He was a believer in will and decision. The party, he thought, had a unique chance for victory by armed action that might never return if allowed to slip away. "To wait is a crime against the Revolution. . . . Delay truly means death."[21]

The actual course of the October Revolution, as I have shown in my own study of those events,[22] was compounded of accidents and ironies. Lenin's lieutenants, including both Trotsky and Stalin, continued to resist the idea of an uprising prior to the Congress of Soviets. Though they voted *pro forma* with Lenin, they confined themselves to defensive preparations until a day and a half before the congress was to convene, when Kerensky's government feebly attempted a preemtive strike on the morning of October 24, 1917. The Bolshevik leadership, working through the Petrograd Soviet, called out their supporters among the garrison and the workers' Red Guards to do battle with the anticipated counterrevolution, and discovered to their own surprise that the whole city of Petrograd was falling into their hands with scarcely a shot. Later that night Lenin came from his hideout to the Bolshevik headquarters in the Smolny Institute to discover that the uprising appeared to be in full swing. From that moment on, the operation was represented as the implementation of his directives, though no documents of a plan or an unambiguous decision to act have ever been found.

Confronted in the actual event with just the sort of armed *fait accompli* that Lenin had urged, the Congress of Soviets split bitterly. Moderate Mensheviks and Socialist Revolutionaries walked out to protest the violent deposing of the Kerensky government, and the stage was then set for civil war and one-party dictatorship. This is not to assert with any certainty that these outcomes could have been avoided, but the events of October 24–25, and the abortive but bloody uprisings of anti-Bolshevik military units in Petrograd and Moscow that followed, in fact committed both sides to an armed resolution of the revolutionary situation. Thus, by a chain of accidents, the new Soviet regime immediately found itself in the violently polarized circumstances of a civil war—a struggle shortly to be extended nationwide.

A great deal has been written about the impact of the Civil War on the early Soviet regime. This vicious two-and-a-half-year struggle has rightly been credited with the militarization of the Soviet Communist Party, with inuring the new regime to terror and cruelty, and with the formation of a new culture of revolutionary violence. It is difficult to conceive of any of the enduring political essentials of the Soviet system without reference to the Civil War experience.

There is no reason to suppose, as some have suggested, that civil war as it developed in Russia was anticipated or envisaged by Lenin. His call to "turn the imperialist war into a civil war" was a rhetorical flourish against non-revolutionary pacifism, and at most meant using World War I to support the revolutionary struggle. The actual conquest of power came much more easily than anyone, including Lenin, could have supposed, though Lenin's dissident lieutenants Zinoviev and Kamenev warned of the risk of provoking civil war when they opposed the idea of an armed uprising. Once in power, confronted with armed resistance by elements of the old army, Lenin was ready for the worst: "Every great revolution, and socialist revolution in particular, even if there were no external war, is inconceivable without internal war, i.e., civil war, which is even more devastating than external war. . . ."[23]

For the first six months of Soviet rule, Lenin's policies in the economic realm (in contrast to the political) were relatively moderate, in line with the old Marxist assumption that Russia was unready for ambitious schemes of socialization. Agriculture, of course, was in a state of anarchy with the culmination of the land seizure movement, which led to a food supply crisis and the institution of requisitioning. Acts of nationalization were confined mainly to the financial system, though private ownership of many enterprises was being rendered fictional by the spread of workers' control on the one hand, and the government's ban on dividend payments on the other. Calling his policy "one foot in socialism," Lenin argued against excesses of "democratization" in industry, defended the retention of bourgeois experts and managerial authority, and made clear his attachment to the principal of top–down authority. "The revolution has only just smashed the oldest, strongest and heaviest fetters to which the masses submitted under duress. That was yesterday. But today the same revolution demands—precisely in the interest of its development and consolidation, precisely in the interests of socialism—that the masses *unquestioningly obey the single will* of the leaders of the labor process."[24]

Civil war on a broad scale did not actually break out until the uprising of the Czech Legion in May 1918 and the Allied intervention that immediately followed. These crises abruptly radicalized the Soviet regime, both in its politics and in its economics. In June and July, with a few provincial exceptions, all noncommunist political activity was outlawed, and the one-party system became a reality. At the same time, on the pretext of saving Russian property from German claims, a program of sweeping nationalization was launched that by the end of the year extended to every craft and trade establishment larger than a family shop.

These quick steps of mid-1918, prompted if not required by military exigencies, contributed to the ultimate form of Soviet socialism more than the entire year of 1917 and all the decades of ideological preparation that preceded it. As he did on other occasions, Lenin seized on the most readily applicable theoretical rationale. ("Truth is not in systems," he wrote in his notes on Clausewitz.[25]) In this case his model happened to be the "War Socialism" of Germany's World War I economy. This example of bureaucratic economic mobilization had begun to intrigue him during his exile in Zurich.[26] In 1918 he made it obligatory doctrine for party members, even though a few left-wing purists continued to protest the trend. Conceding that Russia so far enjoyed only "state capitalism," Lenin asked the Central Executive Committee of the Soviets in April 1918, "What is state capitalism under Soviet power? . . . We have the example of state capitalism in Germany. . . . State capitalism *is our salvation*."[27] The following month he wrote, "Germany. Here we have the 'last word' in contemporary large-scale capitalist technology and planned organization, *subordinate to junker-bourgeois imperialism*. Strike out the underlined words, put in place of the military, junker, bourgeois, imperialist state, a state, but a state of the socialist type, of class content, a soviet state, i.e., proletarian, and you realize the *total sum* of conditions which yield socialism."[28] In other words, simply put leaders in charge who enjoyed the requisite state of ideological grace, and the German bureaucratic model would do perfectly well as the framework of Russian socialism.

Meanwhile, in a life-or-death struggle around Russia's entire periphery, the Communist leaders turned themselves into a military staff, with military expediency and effectiveness as their primary criteria of policy. Trotsky began to build the new Red Army on traditional lines of command and discipline, much to the disgust of purists—the "Military Opposition"—who advocated self-governing guerrilla units in the spirit of 1917. After the attempt on Lenin's life in August 1918, the Cheka was unleashed to pursue Red Terror in earnest. Newly nationalized industries were placed under the direction of the Supreme Economic Council and its various "chief administrations" (*glavki*) in Moscow in order to redirect what was left of the economy in the service of the war effort. Finally, the Communist Party itself underwent a major transformation as its organization and membership were enlisted to further the cause of victory.

In 1917, with its burgeoning membership and the eclipse of discipline by enthusiasm, the party approximated the democratic model expressed by its rules and its jargon more closely than at any other point before or since. In the early months of the Soviet regime, as Lenin and his colleagues settled into their government posts, it was not clear that the party as an institution would become anything other than an opinion-mobilizing and propagandizing body, even if an exclusive one. But with the onset of serious civil war, the party was quickly forged into the country's main institution of power and administration, even more authoritative than the nominal government.

In its new mission of mobilizing Red-ruled Russia for victory in the Civil War, the party turned back to Lenin's organizational vision of 1902. Power shifted from the institutions of government—from the central and local soviets—to the party. Within the party, power gravitated from the membership to the apparatus, from the local level to the center, and from committees to appointed bureaucrats at all levels. These trends were codified in official doctrine at the Eighth Party Congress in March 1919. The congress formally created the Politburo and the Secretariat as the organs of policy and organizational command, and proclaimed, "The party finds itself in a position where the strictest centralism and the most rigorous discipline are absolutely necessary. All decisions of higher jurisdiction are absolutely binding for lower ones. . . . Outright military discipline is essential for the party at the present time."[29]

Pursuant to the party's new military mode of organization, the leadership appointed and transferred personnel as needed, broke up nodules of democratic opposition, and converted nominally elected local party officials into the appointed agents of the center. The apparatus of full-time party officials, euphemistically known as "secretaries," not only became the decisive element in the party in distiction to ordinary members who held other jobs and took orders from party officials; it in fact turned into a new government standing within and behind the nominal government of the soviets. This development, capped by the designation of Stalin as General Secretary in 1922, remains the foundation of the Soviet political structure to the present day. It has survived a turbulent history of succession struggles, purges, and war, ever since Lenin's time.

The militarizing spirit of War Communism was carried to its extreme by none other than Trotsky—not only during the course of the Civil War, but even after the Communists had won. "The problem of revolution, as of war," he wrote in his apology for terrorism, "consists in breaking the will of the foe, forcing him to capitulate."[30] With the enemy collapsing and the economy in ruins, Trotsky wanted to turn the Red Army and its principles of organization to the task of reconstructing transportation and industry. He openly called for the "militarization of labor," "compulsory labor service," and "labor armies." "We can have no way to socialism," he went on, "except by the authoritative regulation of the economic forces and resources of the country, and the centralized distribution of labor-power in harmony with the general state plan."[31] As a prophet of the command economy, Trotsky was truly the first Stalinist.

At the time, little came of Trotsky's schemes. Lenin's New Economic Policy cut radically across the War Communism debates between the militarizers and the democratizers, by calling for a return to the old-fashioned cash nexus as the principle for the organization of labor. With its "strategic retreat" to capitalistic methods of market socialism and the concomitant effort to normalize Russia's diplomatic and commercial relations with the outside world, the NEP represented a major deviation from the militarizing trend in the Soviet economy. The question is still debated among Western observers—and now even among Soviet scholars— as to whether the NEP model might have persisted under sympathetic leadership, or whether it suffered from an inherent incompatibility with Communist principles of government.

In some respects, militarization not only persisted under the NEP but even advanced. Industry, though less subject to orders from the center, settled into more conventionally bureaucratic patterns of administration within enterprises, in accordance with the principle of individual authority (*edinonachalie*). Under the leadership of the flamboyant Civil War leader Tukhachevsky, the Red Army moved away from the territorial militia idea toward strict professionalism. But the key development of these years was the emergence of the Communist Party apparatus as the dominant political force in the Soviet Union. Restaffed and manipulated by Stalin in the course of the succession struggle that began in 1923, the apparatus became a near-perfect embodiment of Lenin's original idea of the party as a corps of disciplined professional revolutionaries operating with a military-style chain of command. Shortly after Lenin died, Stalin undertook his first theoretical pronouncement about the party, and echoed the deceased leader's military metaphors. The party, he said, was "the vanguard detachment of the working class," and the "General Staff" was leading the proletariat to seize and hold power through its "solidarity and iron discipline" and its "unity of will."[32] Battling Trotsky's Left Opposition and then Bukharin's Right Opposition, Stalin's apparatus put these principles into practice to perfect the monolithic organization capable of conducting a new phase of revolutionary struggle.

3. Stalin and the Military Model

In 1929, the era of post-revolutionary retrenchment ended with Stalin's attainment of unchallenged personal power, the forcible collectivization of the peasantry, and the First Five-Year Plan of intensive industrialization. These accomplishments, as I have pointed out already, were no longer really revolutionary but rather postrevolutionary, the typical work of the opportunist dictator who combines elements of the revolution and the Old Regime in whatever manner that he thinks will serve his purpose of personal domination and the power of the state. As Adriano Guerra comments, "The old autocratic state was in fact Stalin's inevitable reference point. The weight of backwardness thus acquired a new value in determining the present. . . . The past tended to reproduce itself, and along with an advance in the economic sectors, to cause a retrogression in the area of social and political liberties in comparison not only with the period of the NEP, but even with the last years of tsarism, to the extent of reviving a conception of the state, that of the tsarist autocracy, that was the negation of the Bolshevik conception."[33] Under Stalin, socialism as the public control of economic enterprise began to play an essentially instrumental role as a system for mobilizing resources to overcome national backwardness and maximize the civilian base of military power. Hence the stress on heavy industry that became a fixed star for the system, set against an appalling neglect for the actual human values that socialism was officially supposed to serve.

Stalin deliberately cultivated a military spirit, appealing to the traditions of War Communism as he embarked on his campaign to transform the country. In terms of propaganda, the period saw a return to themes of class war and political and cultural struggle against alleged bourgeois remnants. In the countryside, there was often literal class war to compel the peasants to accept collectivization and to resettle or liquidate those who resisted too vigorously—the prisoners or casualties of war. Military terminology was introduced everywhere—"shock workers" in industry, "brigades" in agriculture, and "class war on the historical front" as bourgeois culture came under assault. "There are no fortresses which Bolsheviks cannot capture," Stalin declared, taking a line from the radical economist Strumilin.[34]

The institutions of the new era embodied militarization with a vengeance. In the political realm, the military mode was rounded out as Stalin emerged as the supreme "chief" (*vozhd'*) and became the subject of shameless adulation, even though he held no formal government post until 1941. Collectivization of agriculture in the form it took was protested by the Bukharin opposition group as a system of "military-feudal exploitation of the peasantry," harking back to the days of serfdom.[35] In the urban-industrial sector, the practices of centralized War Communism familiar from the Civil War period came back as the plan supplanted the market, small business was renationalized, and trade unions were consigned to the function once envisaged by Trotsky of enforcing labor discipline and rewarding productivity. Direction of labor culminated in the State Labor Reserves set up shortly before World War II—in effect, labor conscription. A further step in the militarization of socialism was the Soviet state's outright consumption of human capital in the nefarious enterprises of the Gulag.

As recent economic studies have shown, under Stalin even the planned economy became less guided by scientific assessments, less balanced, and more the object of essentially military commands.[36] In fact, the First Five-Year Plan was drastically though unavowedly revised when shortages of everything made its targets unrealizable. When sacrifices had to be made, it was light industry and consumer needs that had to give way, while heavy industries and the energy infrastructure were supported in their spectacular gains. Later, the priority of the heavy industrial sector was openly and steadfastly acknowledged, not only by Stalin but by his successors. (Violation of this principle was one of the reasons given for the ouster of Khrushchev's rival Malenkov in 1955.) Meanwhile, "building socialism," as the Soviet regime has described its mission for half a century, lost all real content of progress in social values. "Absolute power," says Branko Horvat, "turned out to be just as counterrevolutionary as successful bourgeois counterrevolutions."[37] Official Soviet history, as Dusko Doder has said, "reads like the annual reports of a construction company."[38]

As Stalin's great industrialization and collectivization drive got under way, he began to justify it in terms that would have sounded familiar to the tsar he most admired, Peter the Great. In 1928 he called for an end to "the age-old backwardness of our country,"[39] and in 1931 he delivered his famous speech on how Russia had been beaten by one foreign power after another "because of her backwardness." "To slacken the tempo," he warned, "would mean falling behind. And those who fall behind get beaten. But we do not want to be beaten." With a nod to Marxist orthodoxy, Stalin went on to say, "In the past we had no fatherland, nor could we have one. But now that we have overthrown capitalism and power is in our hands, in the hands of the people, we have a fatherland, and we will defend its independence."[40] It should be noted that this was before the Manchurian incident of September 1931 first raised the specter of aggression by right-wing imperialist enemies.

By the mid-1930s (not merely during World War II), the virtue of patriotism and the rehabilitation of the military glories of pre-revolutionary regimes became priority themes for Soviet domestic propaganda, as illustrated, for example, by the well-known Eisenstein film epic *Alexander Nevsky* (1938). "The defense of the fatherland is the supreme law of life," a *Pravda* editorial proclaimed in 1934 on the occasion of the reinstitution of the death penalty and collective family guilt for treason or defection.[41] The restoration of formal ranks, insignia, and medals in the armed forces (even medals named after tsarist generals) completed the symbolic synthesis of the traditional and the revolutionary in the military realm.

4. Militarized Socialism and the "Capitalist Encirclement"

The militarization of socialism in Russia did not take place in a vacuum. It was deeply and permanently influenced by the international environment of hostile powers in which the Soviet regime has found itself from its beginning—an environment to which it has contributed significantly itself. Outside studies of the development of the Soviet system usually stress historical, ideological, or personal circumstances, and represent Stalinism as the outcome of these internal factors. But one cannot arrive at a full understanding of how and why the Soviet model of socialism assumed such a highly militarized form without taking into account the traumas and threats—real or imagined—that the Soviet state has experienced since 1917.

The possibility that the nature of socialism was conditioned by a hostile environment could not have existed, according to the Marxist premises that underlay the Bolshevik seizure of power, for the Russian revolution was supposed to inspire world revolution. When this millenarian expectation failed to materialize, the Communists were thrown into a great quandary about "socialism in one country." How could one country, still relatively backward in terms of capitalist industrialization, simultaneously institute socialism, develop its economic resources, and hold off the capitalist powers who had already shown that they were ready to respond to the challenge of revolutionary socialism when they intervened against the Soviet state shortly after its birth?

The particular way the Soviet regime chose to resolve this multiple problem was intimately bound up with Stalin's political triumph and his drive for rapid industrialization. For Stalin, "socialism in one country" became the test case in forging the bonds of political control and party orthodoxy in the discussion of Marxist philosophy. He dismissed the old Marxist doubts expressed by Trotsky and his friends, and simply affirmed that backwardness was no bar to the establishment and survival of a socialist system. Industrialization, rather than a prerequisite of socialism, thus became more a post-requisite—a program to be pursued by means of the socialist organization of national resources with the goal of building the country's economic and military ability to defy the "capitalist encirclement."

The deep impact of the Western intervention and the Russian Civil War in the early militarization of the Soviet system is widely acknowledged. The years of the NEP offered a relative respite from outside pressures as the Soviet government sought security through diplomatic normalization and alliances with such diverse and temporary partners as Weimar Germany and the Chinese Nationalists. The anxiety about a renewal of imperialist intervention that arose towards the end of the NEP was largely whipped up for internal political reasons in the course of the Stalin–Trotsky succession struggle (notably on the occasion of the 1927 war scare vis-à-vis Great Britain), and in the successful effort to impose Soviet control over the foreign Communist parties.

Contrary to most retrospective assessments, no great change in the international environment was behind Stalin's rejection of the NEP and his decisive "revolution from above." These steps were primarily a response to Russia's internal economic problems and to the politics of the succession struggle, at this point (1928–1929) between Stalin and Bukharin. To be sure, Stalin conjured up the vision of a new world revolutionary crisis with the object of discrediting Bukharin and his more moderate sympathizers among the foreign Communist parties. But this line of the "Third Period," so-called, was actually initiated before the Great Depression came along to validate it, just as Stalin's call in 1931 for a massive industrial effort to forestall foreign invasion came before the shadow of Japanese militarism arose to validate that alarm.

Despite Moscow's class war propaganda, trade relations with the outside world during the First Five-Year Plan became more important than in any other era of Soviet history. In short, the most fundamental changes in the direction of militarized socialism were undertaken independently of specific foreign threats and indeed in defiance of elementary considerations of national morale, especially in the collectivization drive. Stalin's revolution must be explained instead as the confluence of diverse internal factors—postrevolutionary politics, economic hurdles, traditions of centralism, and personal ambitions.

Once Stalin's revolution was in place, with the command economy enlisting every last peasant and storekeeper as a private in the army of socialism, the foreign threats that could confirm its necessity in fact materialized. In the purge era, the capitalist menace became inextricably woven into Stalin's system of political legitimization, as the pretext for liquidating his political opponents and as the theoretical excuse for the failure of the state to wither away. The challenge of the Axis powers and the actual life-and-death struggle of the Great Patrotic War did not substantially alter the new Stalinist model of socialism, but only reaffirmed it, justified it, and cast it in concrete for the indefinite future. This was exactly the conclusion that Stalin drew in his famous election campaign speech of February 1946: "Our victory means . . . that the Soviet social order has successfully passed the ordeal in the fire of war and has proved its unquestionable vitality." Specifically, Stalin cited his collectivization policy and the priority given to heavy industry over light industry as the two keys to victory and the foundation of the future economic growth he projected. "Only under such conditions can we consider that our homeland will be guaranteed against all possible accidents."[42]

Stalin relied to such an extent on militant confrontation with outside enemies to justify his system that one is tempted to wonder whether it could ever do without international conflict. Would Stalin have had to create the menace of the infidels if it did not already exist? As it happened, the menace did not need to be invented. As Stalin perceived it, it was unveiled by Winston Churchill in his "iron curtain" speech scarcely a month after the election speech. Denouncing Churchill's "racial theory" of Anglo-Saxon cooperation, Stalin asserted in his rejoinder published in *Pravda*, "There is no doubt that the set-up of Mr. Churchill is a set-up for war, a call to war with the Soviet Union. . . ."[43] Thus Stalin sounded the keynote for the entire era of Soviet-Western relations from 1946 to the present. The constant alarm of "imperialist" threats legitimized the structure and priorities of militarized socialism.

In its congealed form, which has persisted ever since World War II, Soviet socialism represents a militarized system of societal and economic relations both in its organizational structure and in its operational values and priorities. "Owing to the advantages of its economic and political system," says the 1968 textbook *Marxism-Leninism on War and the Army*, "the socialist community can use its resources needed to satisfy its defense needs according to a plan, that is, much more efficiently than the capitalist states."[44] In fact, the system confronts its own population as much as it does the outside world with a siege mentality, where all personal interests and relationships must fit the dictates of military-style social discipline. The authors Milovidov and Kozlov assert, "The economic relations of socialism to a substantial degree enhance the military-economic capabilities of the socialist state above those of the capitalist state which is based on private ownership. The advantages of socialism, as Lenin emphasized, derive from the unity of the people's goals to strengthen the nations's defensive capability, goals which express the interests of all the society, all its groups. . . . The socialist economic system ensures a higher concentration and specialization of production."[45]

5. The Military Model and Totalitarian Mobilization

It will be recognized by now that "militarized socialism" is practically synonymous with Soviet totalitarianism. Apart from familiar notions of political dictatorship, however, the term "totalitarianism" is not very specific. In the economic and social spheres, particularly, "militarized socialism" is a more concrete description of the operation and criteria of Soviet totalitarianism. As militarized socialism, Soviet totalitarianism has gone to further extremes than any other instance of the genus. It is more militarized than any other Communist state with a modicum of independence, and more socialist than any totalitarian regime on the Right.

It is not of great importance to argue how much the literal military interest influences leadership policy in the Soviet Union. In principle the party leadership has been just as interested in the country's military prowess as the generals, even if they might have different tactical priorities. The military have been directly represented in the party leadership for decades; after World War II the uniformed services displaced the trade unions as the third largest category in the Central Committee after the party apparatus and the civil government. But all indications are that the political leadership controls the military so well on the one hand, and shares its attitudes so fully on the other, that no room is left for differences other than those of a very pragmatic nature. According to Milovidov and Kozlov, "The principle of the Party approach means that the very method of organizing the defense of a socialist state must coincide with the nature of socialism; that it must be directed at maximum utilization of the capabilities and superiority of the socialist system. It is indeed here that the essence of the Leninist concept of the inseparable bond between military and socialist power lies. . . ."[46]

Militarized socialism, as Stalin was so well aware, was an effective system (though certainly not the only one) for channeling the resources of a semi-developed country to enhance its military power and maintain what has amounted to a permanent state of mobilization in order to guard against the alleged menace of imperialism. Milovidov and Kozlov assert, "The socialist mode of production makes it possible to create and develop a qualitatively higher, more efficient type of modern military organization, to mobilize the greatest amount of resources necessary for the conduct of war, to secure the highest combat efficiency and morale in the armed forces and inestimable staunchness and endurance in the popular masses at the front and in the rear throughout the war."[47]

All this might have been more or less true of the efficacy of the Stalinist form of socialism up to 1945 or 1953. But by the 1960s and 1970s, when the Soviet Union was reaching a much higher level of industrialization, technological complexity, and educated manpower in its pursuit of superpower status, the advantages of militarized socialism were played out. Hence the growing chorus among Soviet experts about economic reform, incentives, decentralization, and marketizing. This new approach was anticipated in Eastern Europe and China by the 1970s, as programs were worked out resembling the economic mix of the NEP in Russia before Stalin made his total commitment to military forms and methods in civilian society. Such ideas underscore the emergence of a surprising new dialectic, as the success of militarized socialism undercuts its own future effectiveness. The revolution is over, and the time for evolution is at hand if the political powers that be are ready to accept it.

Given the impass that success has brought to the Soviet system, Richard Pipes and others have contended that the Soviet political leadership, refusing to mend its ways internally, will be compelled to seek successes in foreign adventures in order to relegitimize its power and principles.[48] Such conjecture is hard to sustain or refute merely on the basis of a structural analysis of the Soviet system and its problems, but it probably understates the ability of the Soviet authorities to contrive ideological rationales for any kind of policy as circumstances and personalities dictate—be it reform or reaction at home or détente or adventure abroad. *Marxism-Leninism on War and the Army* offers the official disclaimer: "Only the enemies of socialism can stupidly insist on an 'export' of revolution, on an encroachment by world socialism by means of force on the 'free institutions' of the capitalist world. Revolution is not made to order but ripens in the process of historical development. . . ."[49]

The description of the Soviet form of economic and social organization as militarized socialism does not imply a particular view of Soviet foreign policy motivations. To impute to the Soviet leadership a commitment to the forcible export of Marxist revolution would be ironic, considering that the Soviet Union has departed so far from the track of social development envisaged by the progenitors of the revolution. Ever since Stalin's day, Marxist-Leninist theory has been reduced to a ritualistic and self-congratulatory catechism. It is altogether unproductive as a source of meaningful goals, strategies, or even tactical judgments. More plausible, in the light of the Soviet leadership's record of ideological manipulation and reinterpretation, is the image of the Soviet Union as a throwback to deep-seated strivings for national glory and imperial advantage, covered in the deceptive language of Marxism and magnified by the USSR's status as one of the two nuclear superpowers. In this view, Moscow is guided by a set of implicit assumptions derived from Russian traditions, experiences, and leadership decisions. This attitude is expressed through a Manichean "we–they" view of the world, and a compulsive need for internal control and discipline. Little attention is given to the satisfaction of mundane human needs, except for those advantages that the upper-level bureaucracy enjoys in semi-secret.

In this context, militarized socialism is not an end in itself, but rather a political instrument. It is a mode of social organization, functioning analogously to the old society of serfs and nobles, as the most dependable means of sustaining military power and national success against more aggressive or more advanced neighbors. Militarized socialism even served as an instrument for the extension of the Russian military base when it was imposed as a system of imperial control and exploitation on the satellite states of Eastern Europe after World War II, much as it was imposed on the Soviet peasantry earlier.

Militarized socialism was Russia's answer to life without real allies in a hostile world. For the sake of its own maintenance and legitimization, the Stalinist system perpetuated an intense sense of the foreign danger. This has meant not only unending isolation and internal stress, but the provocation or prolongation of foreign hostilities, both of which perfectly serve the regime's political needs. The difficulty of escaping from this dialectic might be a much more serious barrier to real reform in the Soviet system than mere bureacratic resistance to modernization.

Notes

1. Ferenc Feher, Agnes Heller, and Gyorgy Markus, *Dictatorship Over Needs* (New York: St. Martin's, 1983).

2. See, for example, Najdan Pašić, "Suština i smisao borbe Jugoslovenskih komunista protiv staljinizma" (The Essence and Meaning of the Struggle of the

Yugoslav Communists against Stalinism), *Socijalizam* (Belgrade), XII: 5 (May 1969), p. 633.

3. Branko Horvat, *The Political Economy of Socialism: A Marxist Social Theory* (Armonk, N.Y.: M. E. Sharpe, Inc., 1982), p. 56.

4. See, for example, *On Khrushchev's Phoney Communism: Comment on the Open Letter of the Central Committee of the CPSU* (July 14, 1964; Peking: Foreign Languages Press, 1964); and "The Current Danger of War and the Defense of World Peace," *Red Flag*, November 2, 1979 (translated in Foreign Broadcast Information Service, People's Republic of China, November 27, 1979, pp. A1–7), where "the Brezhnev clique" is likened to the tsarist bureaucracy and the Soviet Union is termed "an imperialist superpower wearing the socialist sign." Direct attribution of this behavior to a bureaucratic ruling class was expressed repeatedly in personal conversations by members of the Chinese Academy of Social Sciences in June 1982.

5. Adriano Guerra, *Dopo Brežnev: È riformabile il socialismo sovietico?* (After Brezhnev: Is Soviet Socialism Reformable? Rome: Editori Riuniti, 1983), p. 21.

6. See, for example, J. L. Talmon, *The Rise of Totalitarian Democracy* (Boston: Beacon Press, 1951); and Peter Berger, "Substituting Socialism for God," *New York Times Book Review*, October 9, 1983.

7. Emile Durkheim, *Socialism and Saint-Simon* (1928; London: Routledge and Kegan Paul, 1959), p. 19.

8. Cornelius Castoriadis, *Devant la Guerre* (Face to Face with War, Paris: Fayard, 1981).

9. Quoted in John Wheeler-Bennett, *The Nemesis of Power: The German Army in Politics* (New York: St. Martin's, 1954), p. vii.

10. V. I. Lenin, *What is to be Done?* (1902; New York: International Publishers, 1961), pp. 133, 166.

11. Friedrich Engels, 1895 introduction to Karl Marx's *The Class Struggles in France, 1848–1850*, in Marx, *Selected Works* (New York: International Publishers, n. d.), vol. II, p. 188.

12. See Karl Marx, *The Civil War in France*, ibid., pp. 494–499, and introduction by Friedrich Engels, pp. 458–460.

13. V. I. Lenin, "Two Tactics of Social Democracy in the Democratic Revolution" (July 1905), *Selected Works* (Moscow: Foreign Languages Publishing House, 1950–1952), vol. I, book 2, p. 142.

14. V. I. Lenin, "The Lessons of the Moscow Uprising" (September 1906), ibid., p. 166.

15. V. I. Lenin, "Polozhenie i zadachi sotsialisticheskogo internatsionala" (The Situation and Tasks of the Socialist International, November 1914), *Sobranie Sochinenii* (Collected Works), 2nd ed. (Moscow: Marx-Engels-Lenin Institute, 1928), vol. XVIII, p. 71; and "The War and Russian Social Democracy" (November 1914), *Selected Works*, vol. I, book 2, p. 406.

16. See *Leninskii Sbornik* (The Lenin Collection, Moscow: Marx-Engels-Lenin Institute, 1924–1940), vol. XII.

17. A. S. Milovidov and V. G. Kozlov, *Filosoficheskoe nasledstvo V. I. Lenina i voprosy sovremennoi voiny* (Moscow: Voenizdat, 1972; translated for the U.S.

Air Force as *Philosophical Heritage of V. I. Lenin and Problems of Contemporary War*, Washington, D.C.: Government Printing Office, n. d.), p. 2.

18. Leon Trotsky, "Marxism and Military Knowledge" (May 1922), in Trotsky, *Military Writings* (New York: Merit Publishers, 1969), pp. 110–111.

19. V. I. Lenin, Letter to I. T. Smilga (September 27 [October 10], 1917), *Collected Works of V. I. Lenin* (New York: International Publishers, 1932), vol. XXI, "Toward the Seizure of Power," book 1, p. 265.

20. V. I. Lenin, "The Crisis Has Matured" (September 29 [October 12], 1917), ibid., pp. 227–278.

21. V. I. Lenin, Letter to the Central Committee, Moscow Committee, Petrograd Committee, and the Bolshevik Members of the Petrograd and Moscow Soviets (October 3–7 [16–20], 1917), ibid., book 2, p. 70; and Letter to Bolshevik Comrades Participating in the Regional Congress of the Soviets of the Northern Region (October 1 [14], 1917), ibid., p. 100.

22. Robert V. Daniels, *Red October: The Bolshevik Revolution of 1917* (New York: Scribners, 1967; Boston: Beacon Press, 1984).

23. V. I. Lenin, "The Immediate Tasks of the Soviet Government" (April 1918), *Selected Works*, vol. II, book 1, p. 476.

24. Ibid., p. 482.

25. Quoted by John Keep in "Lenin as Tactician," in Leonard Shapiro and Peter Reddaway, eds., *Lenin: The Man, the Theorist, the Leader* (London: PM, 1967), p. 146.

26. See Alec Nove, "Lenin as Economist," ibid., p. 203.

27. V. I. Lenin, Speech at the session of the VTsIK, April 29, 1918, *Sobranie Sochinenii*, vol. XXII, p. 482.

28. V. I. Lenin, "O 'levom' rebiachestve i o melkoburzhuaznosti" (On Left Childishness and the Petty-bourgeois Quality, May 1918), ibid., p. 516.

29. Resolution of the Eighth Congress of the Russian Communist Party, "Ob organizatsionnom voprose" (On the Organizational Question), *Kommunisticheskaya Partii Sovetskogo Soyuza v rezoliutsiyakh i resheniyakh s'ezdov, konferentsii i plenumov TsK* (The Communist Party of the Soviet Union in Resolutions and Decisions of Its Congresses, Conferences, and Plenums of the Central Committee, Moscow: Gospolitizdat, 1954), vol. I, p. 444.

30. Leon Trotsky, *Dictatorship vs. Democracy* (New York: Worker's Party of America, 1922), p. 54. Originally published as *Terrorizm i Kommunizm* (1920).

31. Ibid., pp. 141–142.

32. Joseph Stalin, "The Foundations of Leninism" (April 1924), in *Problems of Leninism* (Moscow: Foreign Languages Publishing House, 1940), pp. 72–83.

33. Guerra, *Dopo Brežnev*, p. 176.

34. Joseph Stalin, "The Tasks of Business Executives" (February 1931), *Problems of Leninism*, p. 367. Cf. S. G. Strumilin, "Industrializatsiya SSSR i epigony narodnichestva" (The Industrialization of the USSR and the Epigones of Populism), *Planovoe Khoziaistvo*, no. 7, 1927, p. 11.

35. Declaration by Bukharin, Rykov, and Tomsky, February 9, 1929, quoted in the Politburo resolution of the same date, *CPSU in Resolutions*, vol. II, p. 558.

36. See Holland Hunter, "The Overambitious First Soviet Five-Year Plan," *The Slavic Review,* vol. XXXII:2 (June 1973).

37. Horvat, *The Political Economy of Socialism,* p. 46.

38. Dusko Doder, private conversation, April 24, 1984.

39. Joseph Stalin, "Industrialization of the Country and the Right Deviation in the CPSU (B)" (November 1928), *Works* (Moscow: Foreign Languages Publishing House, 1949–1954), vol. XI, p. 259.

40. Joseph Stalin, "The Tasks of Business Executives," *Problems of Leninism,* pp. 365–366.

41. "Za otechestvo" (For the Fatherland), *Pravda,* June 9, 1934.

42. Joseph Stalin, Pre-Election Speech of February 6, 1946, translated in *The Strategy and Tactics of World Communism: Supplement I,* U.S. House of Representatives Document no. 619, 80th Congress, 2nd Session (Washington, D.C.: Government Printing Office, 1948), pp. 170, 177.

43. Joseph Stalin, Answer to *Pravda* Correspondent, *Pravda,* March 14, 1946, translated in *The New York Times,* March 14, 1946.

44. *Marksizm-Leninizm o voine i armii* (Moscow: Voenizdat, 1968), p. 262.

45. Milovidov and Kozlov, *Filosoficheskoe nasledstvo V. I. Lenina,* p. 138.

46. Ibid., p. 260.

47. *Marksizm-Leninizm o voine i armii,* p. 289.

48. See Richard Pipes, *Survival Is Not Enough: Soviet Realities and America's Future* (New York: Simon & Schuster, 1984), pp. 41–44.

49. *Marksizm-Leninizm o voine i armii,* p. 90.

3

Stalinism and
Russian Political Culture

The effort to understand Stalinism and its lingering legacy brings one back time and again to the question, to what extent is it attributable to the perpetuation or revival of old Russian political habits? Further, if this is true to any significant degree, how explain the survival of such traditions through the upheaval of the revolution? The answer to both questions lies in recognizing the force of old, often buried and inarticulate, but nonetheless living political folkways that defy conscious efforts to revolutionize a country's institutions. In other words, Stalinism may be comprehended in part as an expression of enduring features of Russian political culture.

Political culture has emerged in the past few years as one of the most widely invoked concepts in the interpretation of Soviet affairs. But generalities about Russian tradition and national character are not enough to demonstrate how the cultural legacy of the remote past may continue to affect the politics of the present. A ground-breaking effort to do this by identifying the concrete substance of Russian political culture and its influence in the post-revolutionary Soviet Union has recently been made by Edward Keenan.[1] Keenan has brought to light some extraordinary parallels between old—i.e., pre-Petrine—patterns of political behavior and the Soviet *modus operandi*. Indeed, the correspondence is so close that one finds it hard to believe that Keenan did not have the Soviet regime in mind when he constructed his image of Muscovite politics. But in any case, the resemblance between the two epochs implies a powerful carryover of ancient prerevolutionary ways into the postrevolutionary mentality.

1. The Concept of Political Culture

To a student of culture in its proper anthropological sense, the sort of continuity that Keenan depicts in Russian politics is not in the least surprising. Culture, to cite the definition offered by Edward Tyler over a century ago and never improved upon, is "that complex whole which includes knowledge, belief, art, morals, law, custom, and any other capabilities and habits acquired by man as a member of society."[2] The cultural heritage, including political culture, passed from one generation to another by learning or osmosis, is not easily altered except in the most superficial respects.

The notion of political culture first achieved currency in the late 1950s and early 1960s through the work of such political scientists as Gabriel Almond and Lucian W. Pye, primarily with reference to problems of political modernization in the Third World.[3] Its application to Russia and to Soviet studies was undertaken mainly by British political scientists in the 1970s, notably Archie Brown and Stephen White.[4] For the most part, these studies have embraced a narrow or "subjectivist" sense of political culture, confining it to expressed political sentiments, as against the broad or behavioral understanding of culture preferred by the anthropologists.[5] The latter have distinguished "overt" and "covert" or "explicit" and "implicit" culture,[6] thereby taking cognizance of those aspects of culture that lie buried in the implications of people's actions and folkways, as well as what they say about their own behavior. One might invoke here Pareto's contrast of "residues" and "derivations"— on the one hand the underlying modes of behavior embodying implicit culture, and on the other the more variable forms of their overt expression at the self-conscious, verbal level of explicit culture.

As Keenan shows, Russia represents an extreme case in the governance of society by unacknowledged political folkways: "The abiding deep structures of that culture have not found systematic expression either in legislative or in descriptive codifications."[7] Consequently the narrow approach to political culture simply will not do, even if this means that political culture and its influence are rendered even less tractable as objects of scientific testing.

While the political scientists have inappropriately restricted the meaning of political culture in one direction, they have embraced a questionable extension of it in another, to include formal ideologies or "official political culture."[8] Official doctrine may or may not represent a significant policy guide for a revolutionary government, and thus may affect culture, but it is an abuse of the culture concept to stretch it to cover formal ideology. There is, of course, a culture (or sub-culture) of the Communist leadership and bureaucracy, just as there was a Court culture in the old days, but the important thing in getting at the reality of this level of culture is to distinguish it from formal ideology, not to identify the two. For example, the "dictatorship of the proletariat" is ideology, not culture;

but the authoritarianism and reliance on coercion that it meshes with are indeed culture. Similarly with "socialism," as distinguished from its cultural underlay in the Russian antipathy to individual enterprise and reliance on state responsibility.

A common error in the Soviet instance is to assume that ideology represents a set, unchanging cultural force. Much of the early application of the notion of political culture to the Soviet scene cast it as an effort by the Communist regime to inculcate the presumably new and fixed official culture into the populace in place of its old culture.[9] But the reality is more nearly the opposite. The key to understanding the role of Russian political culture under Stalinism and after is to recognize that the operative meaning of ideology has in many respects been changed radically by pragmatic responses to events and by high-level reinterpretation (e.g., regarding Russian nationalism or socio-economic stratification). The reinterpreted ideology itself comes to represent a reflection of or adaptation to the old political culture in a new guise. Mary McAuley quotes Lev Kopelev tellingly to this effect: "The actual ideology of the Stalinists, which still lives today . . . is an ideology of authoritarian bureaucratic party discipline, of superstate chauvinism, of unprincipled pragmatism. . . . In its true essence the Stalinist ideology is significantly further both from the old Bolshevism and even more from all varieties of Marxism, old and new, than from certain contemporary conservative nationalist and religious ideologies. . . ."[10]

The broader conception of culture, including its implicit behavioral manifestations, is not without pitfalls in its application. One is to treat it as a given, outside of time, exempt from historical change; the other is to view a particular culture as a unique entity without comparative associations. Much of what Keenan finds, if we stop to think about it, is only the Russian variant of the values of traditional society in general, including hereditary class status, the political centrality of family relationships, and the need to believe in a personal embodiment of authority.

To correct these limitations we need a more historically oriented conception of political culture as well as of culture as a whole. Political culture should be approached as a system that is both continuous and changeable, that steadily absorbs new infusions from a nation's historical experiences and contacts, while older elements are eroded, metamorphosed, or sloughed off. Political culture builds up and changes like a series of geological deposits. However, it is not always the oldest and deepest elements of a culture that disappear in the face of new experiences: in Russia, in fact, it was the newer, Western-derived elements of the political culture which were most seriously weakened by the upheaval of the Revolution.

2. Muscovite and Soviet Politics

In a wide range of political features, the Soviet regime fits like a glove over the old anatomy of Russian government. In its centralism, in its passion for top-down control, in the distribution of political power at the top and in the style of its use, and in the role of ideological legitimation of the whole, the congruence of the new Moscow with the old one leaps out at the perceptive observer. Many are the visitors, diplomats, and journalists who have commented on the eery similarity of present Soviet practices—secrecy and isolation of foreigners, for example—with old tsarist custom.[11] Stephen White, who deviates from the political science mainstream in his sense for the past, says quite bluntly, "Soviet political culture is rooted in the historical experience of centuries of autocracy."[12]

Where Keenan differs from other observers is in taking the past rather than the present as his point of departure. Instead of projecting a political schema back from the Soviet scene to find past roots or analogues, Keenan goes directly to the past, and lets the evident continuities from then to now speak for themselves. He avoids some of the distortion inherent in present-mindedness, while his own sixteenth-century–mindedness turns out to be highly persuasive.

Muscovy always stood out among early modern states in its degree of centralism and the lack of legal or customary restraints on the despotic power of the tsar. Keenan notes the Russian fear of self-destruction if power were left in local hands, and the importance of preserving the idea of someone at the center who is absolutely in charge. The leap to present-day neo-Stalinism and the yearning for a "tough boss" (*krepkii khoziain*) is not great. "Russia needs a strong autocrat," writes the emigré Yuri Glazov. "*De facto* Stalin did not differ from any strong monarch of pre-Petrine Russia."[13] Keenan observes a continuing Russian need to control and to be controlled, so as to forestall the horror of "chaos." One recalls here the revealing pleas to avoid "panic" broadcast at the time of Stalin's death and again when Brezhnev departed the scene.

One legacy of Russian political culture is an extraordinary internalization of the power of the autocracy among its subjects. As it is described by Piero Ostellino, the long-time Moscow correspondent of *Corriere della Sera*, "The Power anticipates the upsurge of complaints, acting so that the people accept their role in the existing order of things, do not dare to imagine an alternative to such an order, and end by considering it natural and unchangeable. Thus arises the law of anticipated reactions: the man in the street tends to take for granted, even when it does not explicitly exist, the veto of the system over certain behavior. The political-psychological mechanism ends by transforming into consensual power, the overall coercive power of the system, which comes to be considered inevitable and therefore acceptable by getting used to it."[14]

Some of the most intriguing continuities or parallels between Muscovy and the Soviet Union as Keenan draws them forth are to be found in what is not said about the system. Both regimes have been wedded to secretiveness, not only about policy decisions, but about the whole policy-making process as well as the personal actors in that process: "Iz izby soru ne vynesi."[15] For the public, domestic as well as foreign, decisions always have to be made to appear unanimous, masking the actual debate and infighting that goes on within the oligarchy. Shades of "democratic centralism"! Most interesting and provocative of all is Keenan's description of the oligarchic politics of contending clans or clientele groups, covered up then as now by the myth of a political monolith. The picture bears an uncanny resemblance to the image that speculative Kremlinology presents of bureaucratic competition among high party chieftains and their respective groups of followers (*Seilschaften*, "climbing teams," from the analogy with a team of mountain climbers who all depend on the same rope[16]). Power, now as then, resides in concentric circles around the Kremlin, institutionalized today as the Politburo, the Central Committee, and the lesser nomenklatura. It appears that attempts at an "interest group" or "conflict model" interpretation of Soviet politics, or what I have termed "participatory bureaucracy," simply reflect the perpetuation of an old Russian habit of struggling for power and proximity to the Court, under the guise of loyal unity and subordination.[17]

This being the case, one of the highest priorities of both Muscovite and Soviet political culture has been to keep the principles of that culture—the real rules of the game—from being divulged at all. "Those who needed to know such rules knew them, and those who had no need to know were kept in ignorance," Keenan writes.[18] An example that I will elaborate later on is the set of remarkably strict but unwritten rules (Graeme Gill calls them "conventions") that took shape under Stalin to govern the assignment of Central Committee rank to bureaucratic positions, and that incidentally illustrate the perpetuation of the obsession with rank and precedence characteristic of Keenan's Court culture.[19] Unacknowledged but fundamental practices of this nature highlight the true role of ideology for both the Muscovite and the Soviet eras—not a statement of operating principles or goals, but a thick smokescreen to divert attention from the way things are actually done, "to decorate and to conceal the system's essential features."[20] To be sure, neither Russia nor Communism are alone in this ideological hide-and-seek; it is the degree that distinguishes them. So, while formal ideologies should be considered distinct from political culture, the manner of their use is fundamental to political culture.

Along with the Muscovite–Soviet parallel in the political process advanced by Keenan, there is an equally strong continuity in the relationship between the political realm and society as a whole. This revolves around the hypertrophy of the state and society's submission to this fact, stressed by generations of prerevolutionary Russian historians. As Alain Besançon has observed, "Development through coercion—and the substitution of the State for civil society—constituted the historical originality of Russia."[21] Though the two Moscows differ as night and day in literal ideology, they are alike in their use of it—the religious (or today quasi-religious) justification of authority; the political insistence on one correct mode of philosophical belief, served as well by Marxism as by Orthodoxy; and the liturgical, formula-ridden mode of public discourse whatever its philosophical substance. Many of the more peculiar habits of today's government, ranging from the lack of a concept of honorable retirement, to the seclusion of the wives of the leaders, could be traced to Muscovite origins, certainly more readily than to Karl Marx.

Another salient continuity in Russian political culture is the xenophobic attitude toward neighboring ethnic groups and toward foreign nations— specifically, the urge to dominate where it is possible, and fear and suspicion where it is not. Edward Allworth has noted how the ethnic Russians depend on border minorities to cushion them against foreign countries, and from behind this buffer view the rest of the world with "suspiciousness of outsiders, envy, parochialism, intolerance, and above all, unthinking, blind patriotism."[22] The common lament of emigrés that Communism is fundamentally un-Russian[23] misses the point. Russia has russified Communism more than Communism has communized Russia.

3. Political Culture and the Revolution

However compelling all the apparent associations of ancient and recent political culture in Russia, there remains the question of explaining how these folkways could persist through the revolutionary cataclysm of the twentieth century. This task is not as difficult as it might seem if the nature of the revolutionary process is fully appreciated.

Great revolutions typically represent themselves as crusades to uproot all the evils inherited from the nation's past and open the path to a future utopia. However, they come to pass not as simple conspiracies to impose a new and alien ideology (the conservative view shared by Russians like Solzhenitsyn), but as extended crises in the nation's social development, in the Russian case brought on by the late nineteenth-century surge of industrialization. While the Old Regime may be brought down by a fortuitous combination of triggering circumstances, the sequence of upheavals released by the demise of traditional authority is an almost inexorable law of history: the attempt at governance by ineffective moderates; the usurpation of power by radical fanatics, resisted by equally fanatical counterrevolutionaries; the quandary of utopianism and the search for forms of compromise and reconstituted authority; finally, the postrevolutionary dictatorship of the opportunistic strong man who synthesizes the new rhetoric and the old methods.[24] In this context, the resuscitation of old Russian political folkways under Stalin is not only understandable but entirely natural.

Revolution can change culture, especially on the overt level, but not necessarily in ways intended by the revolutionaries. The revolution releases forces for change that have been generated beforehand by the nation's social evolution, and it can rapidly shift what are recognized to be the prevailing political and cultural norms. It can shift them too far, in fact, for the implicit cultural system to sustain them, which accounts for the force typically to be observed in postrevolutionary reactions and the revival of old cultural forms (acknowledged or not) that accompanies them. There is a sort of "return of the repressed" operating here. The Austrian psychoanalyst Karl Federn wrote a book called "The Fatherless Society" when Central Europe was in a revolutionary shambles after World War I, in which he warned of the irrational quest for a substitute authority that would animate people suddenly deprived of the old object of their allegiance.[25] It is perhaps not so paradoxical then, that a recent European observer of the Soviet regime could call it a "non-hereditary monarchy."[26]

The "aberration," as Keenan terms it, in Russia's political life in the first quarter of the twentieth century is no mystery if the circumstances of the revolutionary crisis are taken into account. Prior to the revolution Russia was undergoing an extraordinarily rapid change toward Western models in economy, society, modes of thought, and political practices. Culturally, as Keenan notes, these changes were absorbed from the top down, affecting the worker and peasant masses least. At the same time, the revolutionary movement that launched the Communist dictatorship had incorporated many old Russian forms under new labels—conspiratorial tactics, ideological totalism (including a religion of anti-religion), and anti-capitalism. Alfred Rieber writes, "Even the moderates perceived themselves as the bearers of liberal and humanistic values against the ruthless pretensions of the traders and the factory owners."[27] So socialism had no trouble fitting in with old Russian biases, provided it was socialism organized around the despotic state.

In other respects, the revolution, from the Civil War to the purges, dealt a devastating blow politically and demographically to the most

Westernized, culture-bearing social strata. This was the effect of the "plebeian revolution," according to the thesis of Michal Reiman.[28] Old, unverbalized political folkways were physically brought up into the realm of political life by the new postrevolutionary recruits to the ruling apparatus—the "sons of peasants," as Theodore Shanin has described them[29]—first represented by the former Bolshevik undergrounders who rallied around Stalin in the 1920s, and then by the young worker-peasant activists who moved up to fill the shoes of the purge victims in the 1930s.[30] "At each successive crisis," Jack Gray observes, "there was a choice, and in each case the preferred solution was that which more nearly approximated to Tsarist practices. . . . The Russian political culture provided no effective barriers to the re-creation of an autocracy prepared to control the thought of citizens, maintain power through a system of secret police, and brook no rival power in society."[31] The process is documented in the Communist Party's official decisions, notably the Resolution on the Organizational Question of the Eighth Party Congress (1919) and the Resolution on Unity of the Tenth Party Congress (1921). With the rise of Stalin and the defeat of the more Western-influenced Left Opposition, the Communist Party became, in its tribal-unity mentality, its leader-worship, and its sadistic persecution of deviance, a latter-day embodiment of the political primitivism still latent in modern societies (as other varieties of totalitarianism attest). In sum, the Russian revolutionary experience testifies to the negative effects of an attempt to change a country too far and too fast in ways that run counter to its deep political folkways.

Stalinism, in the cultural perspective, represented the triumph of old Russian forms of latent political culture, dampened down by the "aberration" of Westernism in the late nineteenth–early twentieth-century era, but revived with a vengeance once the movement of the revolutionary cycle reopened the path to the ancient habits. Through the synthesis of new institutions and a new language with old methods and old values that is characteristic of the postrevolutionary phase, the Soviet Union under Stalin experienced the paradoxical reincarnation of old Russia that Kopelev describes so well. In the course of this development, as Keenan points out, the Soviet regime reverted from the optimistic revolutionary view of human nature, requiring only liberation from all those coercive institutions that would "wither away," to the pessimistic view of man embedded in the Russian tradition requiring the intense discipline, stimuli, and coercion that only the all-powerful state could enforce. Such was the direction adopted under Stalin, in every area of social theory and policy practice from education through labor relations to criminal justice. The purges, elevating the sons of peasants to the vacancies left by dead Westernizers, undergirded this cultural counterrevolution with the new bureaucratic recruits whom they put in place.

4. Russian Culture and Soviet Totalitarianism

Given the association of the purges with the comeback of Old Russian political folkways and the termination of Russia's Westernizing "aberration," it seems fair to say that totalitarianism in its extreme Soviet form, Stalinism, is a product of the distinctive Russian political tradition. To be sure, totalitarianism is not unique to Soviet Russia or to the realm of Marxist-Leninist regimes. As the modern form of postrevolutionary dictatorship, totalitarianism encompasses not only Communist regimes, but also cases—Italy, Germany, Spain—where revolution (or the threat of it) resulted in avowedly counterrevolutionary dictatorship. But totalitarianism is not a simple either–or quality as the antinomy "totalitarianism–authoritarianism" implies. The term as it has been historically applied embraces a gradation of cases, varying in the degree of control and coercion exerted by the state over society. Measured on this scale (without any attempt to weigh the degree of cruelty inflicted on external enemies) the Soviet form since the rise of Stalin must be judged the most totalitarian of all known instances. This distinction is underscored by the differences manifested over the past thirty years between the Soviet Union and those of its East European satellites with a Western cultural heritage, where the extremes of Soviet style economic centralization and cultural dictation have never rested well even with local Communists.

The intensity and persistence of Soviet totalitarianism invites a cultural explanation, as the congruence of the revolutionary occasion and the underlying bent of political folkways. Russian folkways in the minds of both rulers and ruled helped push postrevolutionary Russia towards the totalitarian extreme. These mindsets include the compelling tradition of centralism and the lack of a sense of individual, local, or group rights as against the central power; the fear of chaos and the abhorrence of publicly expressed dissent; caution or resignation in the face of questions that the central authority is expected to decide; and xenophobic supersensitivity. The paradox of Stalinism, explicable only in these cultural terms, is its combination of a verbal ideology of Enlightenment optimism, internationalism, and technological omnipotence with a deeply misanthropic and paranoid view of its own human material.

5. Political Culture and the Prospects for Change

If, as Keenan's analysis so strongly indicates, the postrevolutionary regime known as Stalinism has embedded itself deeply in fundamental proclivities of Russian political culture, is there any prospect for democratization of the system? Specifically, can the new leadership around

Gorbachev succeed in pushing through reforms that go radically against old folkways?

Keenan's account of traditional Russian political premises sounds an ominous counterpoint to the catchwords of the Gorbachev administration. Decentralization vs. centralism, *glasnost'* vs. *neglasnost'*, radical restructuring vs. conservative caution, appeals to initiative vs. evasion of responsibility, rejection of the party's infallibility vs. the reassurances of orthodoxy—the reform program could not be couched in terms more antithetical to Russian habits and expectations. It is not hard to understand why Gorbachev's appeal for a new revolution has met with widespread unease and foot-dragging, not only among the bureaucratic special interests, but at all levels of Soviet society.

Two opposite potentialities are exerting their pull today. One is the old political culture of the autocratic tradition, reincarnated in Stalinism and perpetuated in Brezhnevism. The other is the cultural infusion of the period of the "aberration," climaxed by the spirit of 1917 and selectively endorsed on the verbal level by the same Soviet regime that ultimately embodied the conservative authoritarianism of Old Russia. Gorbachev is trying to shift the balance significantly, if not totally, back to the direction of that aberration. But if political culture could subvert the essence of the revolution, what hope is there for an individual reformer, however powerful, to change the foundations of the system?

Not only do Gorbachev's reform efforts appear inauspicious in the light of the cultural heritage that still seems to operate in Russia. The oft-voiced hope that world tensions could be resolved if only the Soviet Union would change—i.e., abjure its Marxist ideology—is rendered hopelessly fatuous. Russia is what it is politically, in its international as well as domestic behavior, for reasons that are far deeper than its ideological language. A switch in languages would only mean a different kind of protective cover for the profound hostilities toward themselves and toward others that seem to govern the Russians' political nature.

Notes

1. Edward L. Keenan, "Muscovite Political Folkways," *The Russian Review*, XV:2 (April, 1986).

2. Edward Tyler, *Primitive Culture* (1871), quoted in Robert C. Tucker, "Culture, Political Culture, and Communist Society," *Political Science Quarterly*, LXXXVIII:2 (June 1973), p. 173.

3. See Lucian W. Pye and Sidney Verba, eds., *Political Culture and Political Development* (Princeton: Princeton University Press, 1965).

4. See A. H. Brown, *Soviet Politics and Political Science* (London: Macmillan, 1974); Archie Brown and Jack Gray, eds., *Political Culture and Political Change*

in Communist States (New York: Holmes and Meier, 1977); Stephen White, *Political Culture and Soviet Politics* (New York: St. Martin's, 1979).

5. The two conceptions of political culture are contrasted by Tucker, "Culture," pp. 176–177, and by Mary McAuley in "Political Culture and Communist Politics: One Step Forward, Two Steps Back," in Archie Brown, ed., *Political Culture and Communist Studies* (London: Macmillan, 1984), p. 14.

6. Ralph Linton, *The Cultural Background of Personality* (New York: Appleton-Century, 1945), p. 38; Clyde Kluckhohn and William H. Kelly, "The Concept of Culture," in Clyde Kluckhohn, *Culture and Behavior* (Glencoe, Ill.: The Free Press of Glencoe, 1962), pp. 62–63.

7. Keenan, "Folkways," p. 116.

8. See Archie Brown and Stephen White in Brown & Gray, *Political Culture*, pp. 14–15, 35–38; Gabriel Almond, "Communism and Political Culture Theory," *Comparative Politics*, XV:2 (January 1983), p. 131.

9. See, e.g., Frederick Barghoorn, "Soviet Russia: Orthodoxy and Adaptiveness," in Pye and Verba, *Political Culture*.

10. Lev Kopelev, "A Lie is Conquered Only by the Truth," in Roy Medvedev, ed., *Samizdat Register*, vol. I (London, 1977), p. 237, quoted by Mary McAuley, "Political Culture," pp. 32–33.

11. See, e.g., Phyllis P. Kohler, ed., *Custine's Eternal Russia: A New Edition of Journey for Our Time* (Miami: University of Miami Center for Advanced International Studies, 1976).

12. Stephen White, "The USSR: Patterns of Autocracy and Industrialism," in Brown & Gray, *Political Culture*, p. 25.

13. Yuri Glazov, *The Russian Mind Since Stalin's Death* (Dordrecht: Reidel/Kluwer, 1985), p. 222.

14. Piero Ostellino, *In che cosa credono i russi?* (What Do the Russians Believe In? Milan: Longanesi, 1982), p. 17.

15. "Don't take your dirt outside the house." Keenan, "Folkways," p. 119.

16. Cf. Gyula Jozsa, "Political Seilschaften in the USSR," in T. H. Rigby and Bohdan Harasymiw, eds., *Leadership Selection and Patron–Client Relations in the USSR and Yugoslavia* (London: Allen & Unwin, 1983).

17. See "Conflict and Authority" (discussion with Carl Linden, T. H. Rigby, and Robert Conquest), *Problems of Communism*, XII:5 (September–October 1963), continued as "How Strong is Khrushchev," XII:6 (November–December 1963); H. Gordon Skilling and Franklyn Griffiths, eds., *Interest Groups in Soviet Politics* (Princeton: Princeton University Press, 1970); Robert V. Daniels, "Participatory Bureaucracy and the Soviet Political System," in Norton T. Dodge, ed., *Analysis of the USSR's 24th Party Congress and 9th Five-Year Plan* (Mechanicsville, Md.: Cremona Foundation, 1971).

18. Keenan, "Folkways," p. 145.

19. See Robert V. Daniels, "Office Holding and Elite Status: The Central Committee of the CPSU," in Paul Cocks, Robert V. Daniels, and Nancy W. Heer, eds., *The Dynamics of Soviet Politics* (Cambridge, Mass.: Harvard University Press, 1976); Robert V. Daniels, "Evolution of Leadership Selection in the Central Committee, 1917–1927," in Walter M. Pintner and Don K. Rowney, eds., *Russian*

Officialdom: The Bureaucratization of Russian Society from the Seventeenth to the Twentieth Century (Chapel Hill: University of North Carolina Press, 1980); Graeme Gill, "Institutionalization and Revolution: Rules and the Soviet Political System," *Soviet Studies*, XXXVI:2 (April 1985).

20. Keenan, "Folkways," p. 145.

21. Alain Besançon, "Soviet Present and Russian Past," *Encounter*, L:3 (March 1978), p. 89.

22. Edward Allworth, "Ambiguities in Russian Group Identity and Leadership of the RSFSR," in Edward Allworth, ed., *Ethnic Russia in the USSR* (New York: Pergamon, 1980), p. 34.

23. This position has been made familiar by Alexander Solzhenitsyn. For a more recent example, see "Yuri Lyubimov, Director in Exile," *The Washington Post*, March 10, 1985.

24. I have expounded this argument in various works. See *The Nature of Communism* (New York: Random House, 1962), pp. 46–68; "Whatever Happened to the Russian Revolution," *Commentary*, LXVI:5 (November 1978).

25. Karl Federn, *Zur Psychologie der Revolution: Die vaterlose Gesellschaft* (Leipzig and Vienna: Anzengruber, 1919).

26. Alberto Ronchey, *Corriere della Sera*, March 12, 1985.

27. Alfred J. Rieber, *Merchants and Entrepreneurs in Imperial Russia* (Chapel Hill: University of North Carolina Press, 1982), p. 424.

28. Michal Reiman, "Spontaneity and Planning in the Plebian Revolution," in R. Carter Elwood, ed., *Reconsiderations on the Russian Revolution* (Cambridge, Mass.: Slavica, 1976).

29. Theodore Shanin, personal communication.

30. See Robert V. Daniels, *The Conscience of the Revolution: Communist Opposition in Soviet Russia* (Cambridge, Mass.: Harvard University Press, 1960), pp. 304–311; Sheila Fitzpatrick, "Stalin and the Making of the New Soviet Elite, 1928–1939," *Slavic Review*, XXXVIII:3 (September 1979).

31. Brown & Gray, *Political Culture*, p. 260.

PART TWO

Bases for Reform

4

The Intelligentsia and the
Failure of Reform: Khrushchev

The historical record as I have examined it thus far casts the prospects for reform in Gorbachev's Russia in a very gloomy light. Experience, institutions, culture all seem to conspire to lock the political life of the Soviet Union in a vise of postrevolutionary despotism. Yet major developments have transpired in Soviet society that have, by fits and starts, activated contrary elements of the Russian tradition. These forces are embodied above all in the Russian intelligentsia, the representatives, if you will, of Keenan's turn-of-the-century Westernizing "aberration."

In Russia, prerevolutionary and postrevolutionary alike, the intelligentsia has been the key to reform. It was the principal constituency for reform under Khrushchev, though neither the leader nor the class had the staying power to carry fundamental changes through successfully in that era. Now, thanks to the transition from Brezhnev to Gorbachev, the intelligentsia has emerged more strongly than ever as the decisive social force on the side of reform. In alliance with the country's political leadership it holds the potential for effecting an epochal new turn in Russia's cultural and institutional foundations.

1. The Intelligentsia as
a Social Force in Russia

For more than two centuries the intelligentsia and the Russian state have co-existed in an uneasy relationship with one another. The state fears the intelligentsia and represses it, but needs it and must cultivate it. As the embodiment of the national conscience and national progress, the intelligentsia represents a commitment to ideas and cultural creation that has perpetuated itself despite all kinds of national upheavals and disasters. "We have dedicated ourselves to a cause, but without hope," wrote Alexander Herzen. "The day of action may still be far off: the day of conscience, of thought, of speech has already dawned."[1] The intelligentsia defies the state, though its powers are sadly inferior; nevertheless, it has always been the source of political change in Russia.

Now the political leadership is turning to the intelligentsia as an ally against the old machinery of political power, in the name of national revival. "No single cause," says the emigré physicist and publisher Valery Chalidze, "can explain the tragic course of Russian history for the last two centuries, but the hostility, the lack of mutual understanding, between the state and the intelligentsia was surely a significant factor. Elimination of this conflict is absolutely necessary for Russia's health in the future."[2]

There are several reasons why the intelligentsia has been a unique force in modern Russian history. It came into being as the embodiment of Western influence—the scientific, literary and political currents that shaped the mind of the educated class from the time of Peter the Great. For the same class it offered a mental alternative to slavish service of state and church. It acquired distinctive prestige vis-à-vis both government and populace because until the late nineteenth century there was no commercial bourgeoisie to speak of to compete with it for influence— a condition to which Russia was returned after the revolution. In Russia the intelligentsia is the only source of articulate national leadership outside of the state power itself. "The intellectuals, the creative segment of the intelligentsia," according to the emigré sociologist Vladimir Shlapentokh, are "the principle group that resists the mythological activity of the political elite."[3] In Boris Shragin's words, "The Russian intellectual is a sighted person among the blind."[4]

The term intelligentsia requires some refinement. In prerevolutionary Russia it connoted that distinctive social stratum who lived by ideas, whether as the creators or the audience. Soviet usage extended it to the entire white collar class: "those who earn their living without manual labor," in the words of the American literary observer Kathryn Feuer.[5] Or as a Russian student once explained to me, "The toilers work much and think little; the intelligentsia thinks much and works little." A current May Day slogan counts them among the three constituent elements of Soviet society: "Hail to the indestructible alliance of the working class, the collective farm peasantry, and the people's intelligentsia."[6] In this diluted sense the intelligentsia or *sluzhashchie* ("employees") now include many millions of families in the social pyramid (one-fourth of the entire labor force, Brezhnev reported in 1981[7]).

Conceived in these broad terms, the Soviet intelligentsia embraces a variety of disparate social elements, ranging from the privileged bureaucracy of nomenklatura rank, through the various managerial and professional specialities of the technical intelligentsia, to the vast army of clerical personnel serving all the branches of the administrative and economic apparatus. Standing aside from this hierarchy, much as it did in tsarist times, is the creative intelligentsia, embracing scientists, writers, and artists, and those few people in the realm of history, philosophy, and social science who exhibit sufficient independence to warrant classification with this group rather than with the functionaries of the regime. To quote Feuer again, it is the class of "library habitués."[8]

The intelligentsia naturally divides along the lines of nationality, although by the time of the revolution intellectuals from the Baltic region, the Ukraine, and the Jewish population were well assimilated into the mainstream of Russian cultural and political life, including the revolutionary movement. Culture, especially literature and history, has been a focal point of nationality sensitivity, and the intelligentsia of the minority areas has borne the brunt of centralist repression during the Soviet era. However, this discussion will mainly be confined to the Russian (or assimilated) intelligentsia.

There is another element of the intelligentsia that is characteristic not only of Russia but of developing countries in general. I have termed this group the "quasi-intelligentsia"—those who aspire to intellectual status but are not really qualified or accepted in creative or technical terms. This is the milieu from which the most radical revolutionary currents have arisen, in Russia and elsewhere. Its pseudo-intellectual features, especially dogmatic attachment to ideology, have colored the Communist regime ever since the revolution.[9]

Can the creative intelligentsia act as a social force? Certainly it has always enjoyed special influence in Russia, whatever its deficiencies of strength or independence. The intelligentsia is like a church, wielding not the power of guns or money, but the power of belief, truth, and argument. The Communist authorities have clearly recognized this power in their efforts to control the thinkers and writers. As Solzhenitsyn put it, "The Soviet regime could certainly have been breached only by literature. The regime has been reinforced with concrete to such an extent that neither a military coup nor a political organization nor a picket line of strikers can knock it over or run it through. Only the solitary writer would be able to do this."[10]

Is the intelligentsia a class, or merely the servant of other classes? The neo-Marxist school of analysis, going back to Trotsky's *Revolution Betrayed*, and before that to Christian Rakovsky's brilliant articles written in exile in 1928–1930, construes the entire Soviet bureaucracy of officials, managers and specialists as (in Rakovsky's words) "a great class of rulers." This "New Class" takes the place of the fallen bourgeoisie, and enjoys the control of state property in lieu of private capital.[11] Anarchists, notably the Pole Jan Mahajski, polemicizing with the Marxists before the Russian Revolution, had even then warned that socialism might eventuate in the rule of the class of mental workers over the class of manual workers.[12] Popularized by James Burnham, Bruno Rizzi, and Milovan Djilas,[13] the argument has been brought up to date by a host of writers, from the East as well as from the West.[14] Antonio Carlo has capsulized the neo-Marxist formulation: "a systematic domination by the collective property of a central political class bureaucracy."[15] Luca Meldolesi has followed the concept of managerial class rule all the way back to Saint-Simon.[16]

These conceptualizations of a bureaucratic-managerial-intelligentsia ruling class do not satisfy those who note how the Soviet intelligentsia or its greater part labors under the oppressive external authority of the party apparatus. Clearly there are two branches of this class in the political respect, a smaller one with the power and a much larger one with its specialized functions. The contrast has been usefully drawn by Svetozar Stojanović of the University of Belgrade as a distinction between the "ruling class" and the "dominant class," applicable to bourgeois as well as to socialist societies.[17] In the Soviet instance the ruling class is the party-controlled nomenklatura, i.e., the upper bureaucracy, while the dominant class, exercising a non-political *egemonia* of values and work style, is the intelligentsia in its various ramifications.

Pursuing the distinction, we can observe a cultural as well as a functional tension between the two groups. The ruling class formed under Stalinism, with its worker-peasant origins, inherited the cultural veneer of the revolutionary quasi-intelligentsia but remains profoundly hostile to the dominant class of the trained and the creative. It effectively embodies the old Russian political culture, set against the tradition of Westernization represented by the intelligentsia. At the same time the ruling class is the repository of official ideology, the false consciousness legitimizing both the rule of the party and the social dominance of the intelligentsia.

The Soviet intelligentsia has not always been united in defense of its political and cultural position. David Joravsky has distinguished within it a variety of political types—the "learned opportunist," the "pliable man of principle," the "ignorant opportunist," the "militant ignoramus" who flourished under Stalin, the "intransigent specialist," and finally the "Varangian," who confronts the regime directly in the defense of free thought.[18] A Soviet scholar, A. I. Volodin, includes in the history of the intelligentsia not only "the social innovators, the committed revolutionaries," but also "the vacillating intelligentsia, the conservative intelligentsia, and the intelligentsia with a minus sign, as it were."[19]

The contest between the ruling class and the dominant class is not altogether unequal, though it is highly asymmetrical. Since the ascendancy of Stalin there has been a profound contradiction of cultures between the two, which explains much of the record of official repression and control that is often superficially attributed to Marxism-Leninism. Faced with the coercive power of the party-state, the police, and the censorship, the intelligentsia has the power of numbers and of indispensability. As Marshall Shatz writes, "The state . . . cannot simply take advantage of its monopoly of political power and crush the educated elite by brute force when it steps out of line without jeopardizing its own goals of modernization and material progress."[20] An astonishing fact of Soviet history has been the resiliency of the creative intelligentsia, and its capacity to resume its traditional role after the long night of Stalinism. Despite the most difficult ordeals of war, revolution, and purge, the intelligentsia has maintained and transmitted its traditions, both through the family and through formal education. The question now is whether Soviet society has reached that stage in its development where the dominant class may be able to shape or replace the ruling class to an extent that may give the country a regime more consonant with its own true needs and resources.

2. The Intelligentsia and the Revolutionary Process

The intelligentsia was both the progenitor and the victim of the revolution. Moving as all revolutions seem destined to do through the stages of liberal protest, radical repudiation of the past, and ultimate reconciliation with national tradition, the Russian Revolution turned finally into a master and adversary of the intelligentsia more implacable than the Old Regime had ever been. Only the long-term progress of modernization, making the intelligentsia more indispensable to the bureaucracy and more capable of asserting itself in non-political ways, has created the possibility of throwing off the burden imposed jointly by Russia's prerevolutionary tradition and by its revolutionary ordeal.

When the revolutionary era began with the abortive protest movements of 1905, the intelligentsia was totally united in support of the overthrow of the autocracy. Then, when the revolution was temporarily set back during the semi-constitutional regime of 1906–1917, the intelligentsia split among those who would pursue the revolutionary struggle, those who would work within the semi-constitutional system, and those who withdrew from politics. On the whole, the creative intelligentsia took the latter path, symbolized by the publication of the *Vekhi* ("Signposts") essays in 1908. Russians in literature and the arts became a major force in the international cultural revolution of modernism. The growing technical intelligentsia mainly took the liberal middle ground with the Constitutional Democratic Party. This left the revolutionary effort supported largely by the elements of the quasi-intelligentsia who remained most strongly wedded to the fashions of the nineteenth century, ultra-radical in politics but relatively conservative in culture.

After the monarchy fell in February 1917, the intelligentsia overwhelmingly favored the Provisional Government. One of the singular things about 1917, compared with most modern revolutions, was the lack of a student movement in support of the soviets. Indeed, the politically most important segment of the student population were the officer-cadets who fought vainly to support the government of Kerensky. Naked class conflict following the Bolshevik takeover, together with the Civil War and the emigration of hundreds of thousands of families, had a devastating effect on the entire educated class, in terms not only of numbers but of its conditions of life and its relationship to the power structure.

Among the victorious Bolsheviks there were profound debates in the early years over what to do with the vanquished intelligentsia. The ultra-radicals, spearheaded by Alexander Bogdanov (a truly creative member of the intelligentsia himself, as philosopher, economist, and scientist), hoped to sweep away the entire heritage of bourgeois civilization and to cultivate a new proletarian culture—hence the name of the organization they set up to bring enlightenment and inspiration to the workers, "Proletcult." The pragmatists, including Lenin and Trotsky, recognized that the new Russia could not function without the technical intelligentsia, and over the protests of the radicals they proceeded to recruit "bourgeois specialists" to serve the Soviet state in every capacity from industrial engineering to military command. Nevertheless, the Communist dictatorship, as Vittorio Strada has observed, was able to accomplish "an inversion of the relationship between politics and culture," turning the latter into "an instrument of manipulation and control."[21]

When the New Economic Policy was introduced in 1921, a modicum of class truce took effect between the Soviet regime and what remained of the intelligentsia. In his last articles of 1922–1923, Lenin underscored the need for a long-term "cultural revolution" to raise the level of the Russian masses, while meanwhile making use of the skills of the intelligentsia. Thanks to the Thermidorean relaxation of the NEP, the creative intelligentsia enjoyed nearly a decade of renewed modernistic creativity and speculative thought, continuing the cultural movements of the prewar years with even more enthusiasm. In a celebrated resolution of 1925 the Central Committee of the Communist Party, though reserving its "infallible" right to judge the class content in artistic works, acknowledged the virtue of "free competition of various groups and tendencies" in the cultural arena. Intimations of things to come, however, could be seen in the official sponsorship of a new, parallel intelligentsia through such organizations as the Communist Academy and the Institute of Red Professors, and the claims of radical groups in the various intellectual areas to represent the true Marxist position.

A new revolution in Soviet intellectual life came in 1929 as one aspect of the postrevolutionary dictatorship imposed by Stalin. This was the point when truly totalitarian control by the party-state was asserted over the economy and over intellectual life. From 1929 to 1932, the line in culture was ultra-radical, and representatives of "bourgeois" thinking in all areas of the arts, history, philosophy, etc., were silenced or jailed in the name of the class struggle, while dogmatically Marxist groups received the party imprimatur as the representatives of *partiinost* ("party spirit") in each field. Former disciples of Bogdanov, notably the historian M. N. Pokrovsky, played a leading role in the enforcement of what they regarded as class art and class truth.

Once the principle of party supremacy in cultural and scientific life and the machinery of its enforcement were established, a series of remarkable changes in the content of intellectual activity was decreed. These shifts, beginning in 1932 in literature and continuing to around 1936 in the various fields of culture and social thought, are even now rarely appreciated. Under the cover of Marxist-Leninist language, the exponents of ultra-revolutionary thinking in each field were systematically purged, and replaced by a highly traditionalist line in practically all forms of cultural activity. In this manner the characteristic synthesis of revolutionary language and traditionalist behavior that distinguishes the era of postrevolutionary dictatorship was carried over into intellectual life in the Soviet Union. The shift was most clearly marked in literature, with the promulgation of "Socialist Realism" in 1934—"national in form, socialist in content," more accurately, bourgeois-conservative in form, nationalistic-propagandistic in content, norms that were soon extended to all the other arts. Decrees on the writing and teaching of history exemplified the regime's new embrace of Russian nationalism and pre-revolutionary traditions of Russian greatness; the historian Pokrovsky had to be purged posthumously to discredit his ultra-Marxist materialism. Modernism in the arts was condemned as bourgeois decadence, and the environmentalist reductionism in the social sciences that explained individual shortcomings as consequences of the social system was repudiated. As a result, serious work in the social sciences and philosophy, and even genuine Marxist thinking about law and economics, were virtually stamped out. The educational system was rudely redirected from liberationist and polytechnical experiments to classical models of academic discipline.

The events in Soviet cultural life between 1932 and 1936 amounted to a *de facto* counterrevolution, in which the revolutionary intelligentsia was crushed and humiliated as much as the bourgeois intelligentsia had been in 1918–1921 and 1929–1932. Then came the physical decimation of the country's intellectual and political leadership in the purges, the nearest thing to an overt counterrevolution that postrevolutionary Russia has experienced, though it was carried out in the name of Marxism-Leninism and the class struggle.

Stalin's regime was utterly unique, in its time, in the utilization of a revolutionary ideology to legitimate a postrevolutionary and in many respects even counterrevolutionary order. The deception was facilitated by the unusual course followed by postrevolutionary Russia where changes from one phase to another, usually marked by violent coups in the course of the other great revolutions, were accomplished by the revolutionary leaders themselves. Both Lenin in 1921 and Stalin in 1927–1929 and again in 1934–1938 successfully maintained the overt continuity of the ruling party and its ideology while radically changing their policies and their subordinate personnel to carry the country from revolution to retrenchment and thence to despotic internal aggression and counterrevolutionary consolidation.

Unfortunately the price of sustaining Marxist legitimation in support of these successive transformations was the imposition of total party control over all manifestations of social thought and cultural activity, to preclude any challenge of the discrepancy between theory and reality. In Strada's words, "Politics in the USSR overwhelms culture, emptying it of any authentic creativity."[22] The creative intelligentsia, more than any other social element, was crippled and humiliated by the rigors that Stalinism required for its maintenance and self-justification, even apart from the absurd personal glorification on which Stalin insisted more and more as the years went by. "We all have a dogmatist sitting inside," the novelist Chinghiz Aitmatov wrote recently. "We have all suffered a 'concussion' of the Stalinist epoch to a certain extent, weaned from thinking and acting without permission from above."[23]

In broad class terms the intelligentsia, or more accurately the technical intelligentsia, did not do so badly under Stalinism. In the proceedings of the iconoclastic Gramsci Institute conference of 1978 on the history of the USSR, Bertolissi, Bettanin, and Sestan described "the attempt to institute a privileged and selective relationship between the Soviet power and the new scientific-technical intelligentsia composed of technicians 'promoted' . . . from the ranks of the workers and peasants."[24] One may conceive of a contest between the political class and the creative intelligentsia for hegemony over the technical intelligentsia. Stalin won the contest decisively, not only by his use of the police to crush political and cultural resistance, but by tailoring his cultural counterrevolution, including nationalism, the legitimation of inequality, and the repudiation of modernism, to the tastes and interests of the growing technician–office worker class.[25] Meanwhile, at the political level, the purged governing class, also renovated with new recruits from the working class and peasantry, was infused with the pure essence of old Russian political culture, distinguished by secretiveness, authoritarianism, nativism, and anti-intellectualism. This was the "Russianism" still observed by the recent Moscow correspondent of the *New York Times*, David Shipler, "unalterably opposed to pluralism."[26] Stalin had achieved what his tsarist predecessors could only wish for: a class of specialists trained in Western technique, but effectively shielded from the creative and hence threatening thought and expression that Western contacts had always encouraged.

This state of affairs could not go on indefinitely, as modernization turned the Soviet Union into a more sophisticated and aspiring society and as the underground roots of the intelligentsia began to flow with life again. There was an unresolved tension in the absurd disparity between Soviet ideology and reality, between the postrevolutionary regime and its revolutionary origins. By the time of Stalin's death, the progress of modernization had made the Soviet Union ripe for fundamental reform.

3. The Post-Stalin Succession and the Window of Reform

Reform remained unthinkable in Russia as long as Joseph Stalin lived and perpetuated his postrevolutionary despotism by personal terror. His death immediately opened the door to the potentiality of Russia's overdue return to the spirit of the democratic revolution. Yet, given the pervasiveness of the control apparatus inherited from Stalin and the political weakness of the reformist elements, the question whether reform would be implemented or stifled continued to depend on the politics of high leadership and the whims and tactics of those who aspired to inherit Stalin's power. Giuseppe Boffa comments, "Khrushchev's iconoclastic denunciation was the only critique of Stalin that Stalin had left the USSR capable of."[27]

Post-Stalin Russia bore a tense and unnatural relation to its revolutionary heritage, a relation calling for radical changes to relieve the country of the burden of postrevolutionary despotism and the crippling weight of pseudo-revolutionary orthodoxy. In no area was this need more pressing than in the realm of intellectual life. This is why the possibility of reform was met with such enthusiasm on the part of the Soviet intelligentsia, and why the reactions of dissidence and demoralization followed upon the failure of reform.

When the opportunity for reform finally came, it was the creative intelligentsia alone of all the elements of Soviet society which had the interest and the awareness to press for fundamental change. But it was a thin and delicate social stratum, hamstrung by political pressures and the lack of free access to its potential mass audience. The rigors of two decades of repression and official mendacity under Stalin had left the creative intelligentsia in a crippled and demoralized state, particularly so in the fields of history, social science, and speculative thought. Natural science, shielded by its own internal rigor, suffered less, though the shadow of Lysenkoism in genetics loomed large. Under Soviet conditions critical minds have always found a safer haven in the natural sciences, and it is no accident that dissidents of the stature of Andrei Sakharov, Alexander Solzhenitsyn, and the Medvedev brothers should have emerged from the scientific or mathematical milieu. It was the field of literature, however, that by tradition and by its own irrepressible dynamism stood out as the source of reformist energy while reform was still a possiblitity, and as the reservoir of political dissent when a new freeze followed the years of the thaw.

If the critical intelligentsia was the social embodiment of the push for postrevolutionary reform, its natural adversary was the bureaucracy of the party and state nomenklatura, together with its careerist hangers-on in the intellectual professions. Presiding over the postrevolutionary social order, the bureaucracy had a vested interest in the system of controls that both necessitated and sustained its own role in the system. There was, and there still remains, a natural tension between this ruling class of political controllers and all those who attempt to contribute to society through their personal creativity or expertise. Just as the critical intelligentsia was the natural force behind post-Stalin reform, so the bureaucracy was the natural supporter of the unreformed status quo.

For a time, thanks to his strength of personality, Khrushchev was able to pursue a middle road between the social forces of reform and conservatism. This delicate balance was responsible for the spectacle of repeated and confusing shifts in the party line toward intellectual life between 1953 and 1964. But eventually, so strong were the interests of institutionalized Stalinism that even the supreme leadership proved unable to carry through the reform demanded by Russia's postrevolutionary condition and the national conscience. The result of the bureaucratic victory was another quarter-century of suspended political animation, as the country postponed its day of reckoning with the revolutionary legacy, and struggled on toward modernity with its intellectual brakes on.

The impetus to reform showed itself immediately upon Stalin's death. At the political level, receptivity to reform was immediately signalled by the affirmation of collective leadership, curbs on terror tactics, and economic concessions to consumers and farmers. In intellectual life, with "a great surge of renovation," to quote Isabel Esmein in the *Cahiers du Monde Russe*,[28] writers themselves quickly staked out their claims to creative freedom as the sine qua non of a cultural revival. This was in fact the "thaw," the dramatic unfreezing in the cultural climate so named from Elya Ehrenburg's mediocre but timely new novel by that title.[29]

At the outset there was no particular association of the cultural thaw with the personality of Khrushchev. If anyone stood out as an early supporter of cultural renovation it was Georgi Malenkov during the two years of his tenure as Chairman of the Council of Ministers. This was sensed by Soviet intellectuals, who even found support for the reform line in Malenkov's report at the last (1952) party congress under Stalin, when he had called upon literature and art to "burn away everything that is undesireable, rotten and moribund, everything that retards our progress."[30] Robert Conquest concludes in his intensive study of the politics of the succession, "We can with great probability link Malenkov with a tentative patronage of the thaw tendency."[31]

It is ironic in retrospect that Khrushchev's campaign for power against Malenkov was initially associated with the conservative position, in ideological issues as well as in economics and military policy.[32] One of the earliest signs of Malenkov's slippage was the August 1954 meeting of the presidium of the Writers' Union, following which the liberal journal *Novyi Mir* was censured for deficient ideological content, and its editor Alexander Tvardovsky was removed.[33] The long-heralded Second Congress of Soviet Writers in December 1954 (a full twenty years after the first) affirmed this temporary conservative reaction with a sharp attack on Ehrenburg's alleged political deficiencies in *The Thaw* (though in a gesture of balance Tvardovsky was elected to the presidium of the congress).[34]

By the beginning of 1955, through the exercise of the appointment power of the party secretariat, Khrushchev had built a sufficient political base to challenge Malenkov directly. In February of that year he compelled his rival to relinquish the chairmanship of the Council of Ministers to Nikolai Bulganin. With this success behind him, Khrushchev then coopted the liberal position on all the issues, foreign and domestic, that he had used against Malenkov, and proceeded with the political and ideological groundwork for the spectacular Twentieth Party Congress scheduled for February 1956. It would appear that Khrushchev was capable of adopting and discarding issues for reasons of simple political expedience, recalling what Bukharin said of Stalin many years before, "He changes his theory according to whom he needs to get rid of."[35] This trait was to appear again when Khrushchev came under political siege by the neo-Stalinist opposition in the early 1960s. But for the moment, it is significant that Khrushchev saw the embrace of reform as politically expedient, whether for its long-run contribution to Russia's future development or simply as a device to provoke the rest of his old Stalinist rivals in the Politburo to show their hand and submit to a test of strength with him.

The Twentieth Congress was the critical event signalling Russia's tentative emergence from its burden of despotism. For Russia, the congress and Khrushchev's de-Stalinization program that followed meant the repudiation of the personal terror that had cast its shadow over the country for two decades. The impact on the unity and confidence of the international Communist movement, not to mention the relations of the USSR with its East European satellites, was devastating and irreversible. But the Twentieth Congress did not accomplish fundamental changes in the Soviet political and economic system. It was only a potential turning point, whose promise of reform was soon betrayed, and left unfulfilled almost to the present moment.

The intelligentsia as an issue did not figure prominently at the Twentieth Congress, marked as it was by the sensational political issues of peaceful coexistence, the cult of personality, and the selective rehabilitation of the victims of Stalin's purges. Khrushchev devoted only a very brief section of his day-long report to intellectual life, with the commonplace observation, "Our literature and art still lag far behind life, behind Soviet reality." Straddling the line between liberalism and conservatism, he warned, "The Party has fought and will continue to fight against untruthful representation of Soviet reality, against attempts to varnish it or, on the contrary, to scoff at and discredit what the Soviet people have achieved."[36] The dismal intellectual heritage of Stalinism was more directly addressed by Anastas Mikoyan in the speech that presaged Khrushchev's own Secret Speech, lamenting theories that were "lagging behind life," and "the atmosphere that surrounded scientific and ideological work during a number of past years."[37] Even Sholokhov, the one well-known writer to be tapped for an address to the congress, and scarcely noted for his liberalism, attacked the secretary of the Writers' Union and supported the complaints of Khrushchev and Mikoyan: "Our prose has been in a disastrous state in recent years."[38]

While cultural issues remained marginal at the congress itself, the impact of the congress and the de-Stalinization campaign on intellectual life was electrifying. Ordinary Soviet citizens, as I observed myself during a visit in August and September 1956, believed their country had taken a quantum leap toward freedom. In the literary world, Edith Frankel comments, "It was a period of extraordinary vitality. Great hopes had been inspired by the Twentieth Congress and were nurtured in the ensuing months by rehabilitations and other liberalizing measures. It was a time for pulling manuscripts out of the drawer and for sitting down and writing what might have been unthinkable only months before."[39] Wrote Solzhenitsyn, "We began to emerge from the black, bottomless waters and much sooner than I had expected, to emerge in our own lifetime."[40]

4. The Intelligentsia and the Ascendancy of Khrushchev

In the months immediately following the Twentieth Congress the new mood of intellectual liberation had strong official encouragement. The journal *Voprosy filosofii*, to cite one striking example, harked back to the famous 1925 Central Committee resolution against party dictation in matters of literary form, denounced "the transformation of individuals' opinions into guiding ideas," and affirmed the principles of "free competition" and "self-government" in the arts.[41] Assuming that political dictation in the arts had gone the way of the discredited cult of personality, the Moscow writers in particular rushed to bring out a flood of new works, new journals, and new translations.[42] Boffa, at the time the Moscow correspondent for *L'Unità*, hailed "the recovery of the entire cultural patrimony of the Soviet people, all its experiences from the Revolution to the present day, including those experiences which had been arbitrarily set aside."[43] The playwright Kron wrote in *Literaturnaya Moskva*, "The cult is incompatible with criticism; the healthiest criticism is easily twisted into a heresy. . . . Where one man owns the truth uncontrolled, artists are relegated to the modest role of illustrators and singers of odes."[44] Most controversial of all in this literary season was the publication of Vladimir Dudintsev's novel *Not by Bread Alone*, stirring both liberal and conservative passions with its realistic tale of a Soviet inventor's tribulations at the hands of the bureaucracy.[45]

Despite Khrushchev's sensational campaign of de-Stalinization commencing at the Twentieth Congress, neither his political command nor the spirit of liberalization in intellectual life were at all assured. In the following months there were many signs of resistance by the hard-liners of Stalin's former entourage, until the contest came to a head in the crisis of June 1957. In the meantime, Khrushchev seems to have compromised and maneuvered from month to month, beginning with the Central Committee resolution of June 30, 1956. This clearly regressive statement toned down the critique of Stalin and rejected foreign Communist suggestions (particularly that of Palmiro Togliatti) that the evils of Stalinism had deeper roots than Stalin's personality alone.[46] A month previously, Khrushchev had removed Molotov from the Foreign Ministry and replaced him with the Secretariat member and former *Pravda* editor

Dmitri Shepilov. The move put foreign policy in the hands of a presumed supporter of peaceful coexistence, but allowed Molotov to take the lead in cultural matters and impose some restraint on the enthusiasts of free creativity.[47] This was the background of *Novyi Mir's* rejection of Pasternak's *Doctor Zhivago* in September.[48]

A more serious setback to the prospects for fundamental reform in Soviet intellectual life was the crisis in Eastern Europe in the fall of 1956. Khrushchev evidently felt constrained to allow the party conservatives to reassert the principle of control, as Molotov did at a Ministry of Culture conference on the arts in November.[49] Ominous references were made to Andrei Zhdanov's campaign against deviation in literature back in 1946.[50] As Isabelle Esmein explains Khrushchev's ambiguity on the intellectuals throughout his tenure of office, "The First Secretary gives the overall impression that while trying to maintain the authority of the party, he really wants to allow certain forces that strive to play a role in Soviet society, to express themselves." But in the event of "confrontations between these forces and the apparatus . . . he is compelled, when these confrontations run the risk of taking on dangerous proportions, to defend the party resolutely."[51]

During the following months, when Khrushchev's struggle with the Stalinists was approaching its climax, the party line in the arts stiffened further. A curious role was played in this interval by Shepilov, who was brought back from the Foreign Ministry to the Secretariat in February 1957, to take charge of culture. In appearances before the composers and the artists he reaffirmed the supremacy of the party, yet one of the charges against him after the defeat of the "Anti-Party Group" was "a liberal position contrary to Leninist principle, . . . a platform 'wider' than that of the Party."[52] Khrushchev himself twice addressed meetings of the writers in May, to underscore the positive as well as the negative side of Stalin's rule and to complain of those who overreacted to de-Stalinization: "[They] began to vilify and smear workers in literature and the arts who had glorified the successes our people achieved under the Party's leadership. They invented and launched the abusive label of 'pretifier,' pinning it on all who wrote the truth about our reality, about our people's creative labor and great victories. . . ."[53] The July editorial in *Kommunist* went even further, to link literary laxity with "counter-revolutionary" movements such as the uprising in Hungary.[54] Debating a Soviet spokesman about the new trends, Ignazio Silone observed, "These tender shoots of artistic freedom seem to have been blasted by a new spell of Siberian cold."[55]

Nevertheless, the political climate surrounding Soviet intellectual life began to change once again, after Khrushchev prevailed over the Stalinists' attempt to unseat him in June 1957, and removed the "Anti-Party Group" of Molotov, Malenkov, and Kaganovich, "and Shepilov who joined them," from all their positions of power. From this point on, with minor ups and downs (notably the furor over Pasternak's Nobel Prize), conditions gradually improved as long as Khrushchev was in the political ascendancy.

One milestone was the reinstatement of Tvardovsky as editor of *Novyi Mir* in July 1958. This step was followed by his designation to speak at the Twenty-First Party Congress (in late January and early February, 1959). Tvardovsky's speech, condemning the sterility of much contemporary writing and extolling the individuality not only of the author but of the reader as well, was perhaps the supreme document of the era of the Thaw in Soviet intellectual life. He even chided the Komsomol boss (and later KGB chief) Semichastny, a notorious Stalinoid:

> Perhaps, upon hearing the partiality with which I speak of Soviet readers' private libraries, Comrade Semichastny, who delivered a fine speech here, will accuse me of advocating private property and will place the words 'my book,' 'my library,' in the same bracket as 'my car,' 'my country cottage.' But I am prepared to affirm that we can enter communism confidently and unafraid with this particular 'survival' form of property. (Laughter, applause)[56]

The years 1959 to 1962 were, relatively speaking, a golden age in Soviet intellectual life. Khrushchev himself appeared at the Third Writers' Congress in May 1959, to set the tone of intellectual détente with a folksy lecture on boring books. He reaffirmed the principle of party guidance but ousted the conservative Surkov as Secretary of the Writers' Union.[57] As a symbol of the good fortune of the intelligentsia, Tvardovsky's star continued to rise; at the Twenty-Second Party Congress in 1961, he was not only selected again as a speaker but elected a candidate member of the Central Committee of the Party. Meanwhile, remarkable works saw the light of day. Ehrenburg's memoirs, published in *Novyi Mir* beginning in August 1960, have been likened to Khrushchev's Secret Speech as a revelation of the cultural crimes of Stalinism.[58] Yevtushenko's memorable attack on anti-Semitism, "Babi Yar," appeared in the very official *Literaturnaya Gazeta* shortly before the Twenty-Second Congress.[59] A year later came the most sensational publishing event of the whole era of the Thaw, the appearance in *Novyi Mir*, with Khrushchev's personal imprimatur, of Solzhenitsyn's exposé of prison camp life, *One Day in the Life of Ivan Denisovich*.[60]

Abraham Rothberg, following Peter Benno, suggests that Khrushchev intended the publication of *Ivan Denisovich* as a blow against the neo-Stalinists in the party leadership.[61] If so, it was insufficient to keep the political ground from shifting under his feet. The era of the Thaw and the whole opportunity for lasting reform in Soviet political and intellectual life were coming to a disappointing and dispiriting end.

5. The Bureaucratic Resurgence and
the Failure of Reform

The real question about the Khrushchev era is not why reform was attempted, but why it failed. Of Khrushchev, the poet Andrei Voznesensky recalls, "I could not understand how one person could combine both the good hopes of the 1960s, the mighty sweep of transformations, with the impediments of old thinking."[62] From the time of his ascendancy in 1955 Khrushchev set himself against the historical anachronism of Stalinism as he endeavored to revive the early revolutionary spirit and to repudiate Stalin's personal despotism. However, he was cautious and inconsistent in recognizing the intelligentsia as the key force for change, though they were responding to the Thaw with enthusiasm and renewed creativity.

For all his devotion to attacking the Stalin cult and loosening old strictures on the intelligentsia, Khrushchev did not succeed or even attempt to bring about a fundamental change in the Soviet power structure. Boffa describes "an embryonic, but distinct, pluralism of voices, a new and exciting phenomenon," such had not been seen in Russia since the 1920s, but now "an anomaly in a state which orthodoxy wanted to be monolithic."[63] Despite the special prestige that it enjoyed in the Soviet context, the intelligentsia did not become a sufficiently strong and independent social force to compel the political authorities to respect its interest in a true return to the democratic beginnings of the revolution. As events throughout the 1950s and 1960s showed, it remained at the mercy of the political leadership and the shifting winds of factional struggle. The decisive social force, supporting and limiting the leadership, continued to be the conservative bureaucracy, whose interests dictated the avoidance of fundamental reform as long as possible.

Unfortunately for the immediate prospects of reform, the bureaucratic leadership was relatively youthful, having started to climb the ladder of power only after the purges of the 1930s had eliminated most of the older generation of Communists who stood in their way. Whereas the initiative in de-Stalinization came from older top-level associates of Stalin—from Malenkov in a tentative way and dramatically so from Khrushchev and Mikoyan—their younger colleagues of the generation of Mikhail Suslov, Frol Kozlov, Alexei Kosygin and Leonid Brezhnev, all born after 1900, were the immediate beneficiaries of Stalin and Stalinism. Their worker-peasant background and narrow education made these neo-Stalinist representatives of Reiman's "plebeian revolution" a ready chorus for Stalin's anti-intellectualism.[64] As living embodiments of old Russian political culture, they had little interest in changing the rules of the game while they looked forward to many more years growing old in office.

Once Khrushchev's reformist leadership faltered, and the younger representatives of the Stalinist bureaucracy took over, the cause of reform inherent in the logic of the revolution was doomed for another generation. Against the nomenklatura and its physical arms, the police and the censorship, the intelligentsia was helpless to put up direct resistance. They could only turn—that is, the bolder and more alienated among them—to the equivalent of intellectual guerrilla warfare. This was the origin of the dissident movement, in all its varied currents, that has marked the Soviet scene ever since Khrushchev's fall.

It is clear in retrospect that Khrushchev never enjoyed the degree of personal dominance that outside observers credited him with after 1957. He always had to contend with conservatives in the party leadership, even including younger people whom he initially promoted. His policies in cultural matters were always affected by these circumstances, though not in any consistent direction. At times he took the liberal line to provoke or embarrass the conservatives, and at other points he tried to appease them with affirmations of the party's guiding role. He reportedly told the Central Committee in November 1962, "I favor greater freedom of expression, since the level we have achieved in the economy and technology demands this. But some of my colleagues in the Presidium think we must be cautious. Obviously we shall have to wait a while before going ahead any further."[65]

I have argued elsewhere that as early as the winter of 1959–1960, Khrushchev came under pressure from the neo-Stalinists led by Suslov and Kozlov. This circumstance may well account for some of his "harebrained schemes" and his abrupt shift to a confrontational foreign policy after the U-2 Affair of May 1960.[66] In cultural matters, however, Khrushchev found it possible and expedient to hold the liberal course against his opponents, until the shattering events that commenced in December 1962.

The U-2 Affair of Soviet intellectual life was the exhibit of contemporary painting that opened in Moscow's Manezh gallery (the former imperial riding-hall just off Red Square) on December 1, 1962. Khrushchev, still smarting from the embarrassment of the Cuban Missile Crisis, toured the show and launched into a vulgar tirade against the abstractionist paintings that had been included (for the first time since the rise of Stalin). "This is just a mess. . . . Judging by these experiments, I am entitled to think that you are pederasts, and for that you can get ten years. . . . Gentlemen, we are declaring war on you."[67] What followed, in the press and in top-level meetings of the leadership and the intellectuals, was a torrent of denunciation of the liberal heresy in all the arts, including many of the works just recently published with official sanction. The chorus of neo-Stalinist orthodoxy hit a crescendo for the time being when Khrushchev addressed a major conference of intellectuals in March 1963. Now he ostentatiously called a halt to de-Stalinization and turned sharply against those writers, notably Ehrenburg and Yevtushenko, whom he had been supporting in their revelations of past evils. "The press, radio, literature, painting, music, the cinema, and the theater are a sharp ideological weapon of our Party," Khrushchev affrmed in best Zhdanovite style. "The Party will not allow anyone to blunt this weapon or weaken its effect."[68]

Despite these alarming signals, one more reprieve awaited the liberal intelligentsia. In mid-April 1963, Khrushchev's chief neo-Stalinist challenger, Second Secretary Frol Kozlov, suffered a heart attack that removed him from political life and ultimately proved fatal. Relieved of pressure from the conservatives for the moment, Khrushchev reversed himself once again in cultural policy as in foreign policy, and liberal views were allowed to compete with the orthodox for a few months more. Tvardovsky actually campaigned to get Solzhenitsyn the Lenin Prize, though this went beyond what Khrushchev was willing or able to carry through. Solzhenitsyn took the party veto of his candidacy in April 1964 as the beginning of the end for "The Man" Khrushchev. Tvardovsky spoke in German to break the bad news: "Das ist alle. Ich sterbe."[69]

Thereafter the neo-Stalinist conspiracy against Khrushchev rapidly took form for the denouement of October 1964. The intelligentsia did not at first recognize the dismal implications of this event, and continued to press for broader latitude in their publications. Only by the summer of 1965, after a sweeping repression of alleged nationalist intellectuals in the Ukraine, did it become clear that Brezhnev and Kosygin represented a fundamental rejection of the whole era of the Thaw in intellectual life. The decisive event was the arrest on September 8, 1965, of two imaginative young writers, Andrei Sinyavsky (pseudonym "Abram Tertz") and Yuli Daniel (pseudonym "Nikolai Arzhak"), for the crime of publishing anti-Soviet literature abroad. Their trial and sentencing were symbols internationally of the triumph of official neo-Stalinism over Soviet intellectual life for another generation to come. For the intelligentsia the era of hope symbolized by the Twentieth Congress had closed; the pathetic era of subterranean dissidence had begun.

Notes

1. Alexander Herzen, "The Russian People and Socialism: An Open Letter to Jules Michelet," in Herzen, *From the Other Shore* (London: Weidenfeld and Nicolson, 1956), pp. 199, 203.

2. Valery Chalidze, "Andrei Sakharov and the Russian Intelligentsia," speech to the Sakharov Symposium of the American Physical Society, January 26, 1981, reprinted in Edward D. Lozansky, ed., *Andrei Sakharov and Peace* (New York: Avon, 1985), pp. 308–309.

3. Vladimir Shlapentokh, *Soviet Public Opinion and Ideology: Mythology and Pragmatism in Interaction* (New York: Praeger, 1986), p. 45.

4. Boris Shragin, *The Challenge of the Spirit* (New York: Knopf, 1978), p. 153.

5. Kathryn Feuer, "Russia's Young Intellectuals," *Encounter*, VIII:2 (February 1957), p. 10.

6. *Pravda*, April 19, 1987.

7. L. I. Brezhnev, Report of the CPSU Central Committee to the 26th Congress of the CPSU, *Pravda*, February 24, 1981. Here and subsequently where recent Soviet statements are cited I have utilized the *Current Digest of the Soviet Press* as a guide.

8. Feuer, "Russia's Young Intellectuals," p. 11.

9. See Robert V. Daniels, "Intellectuals and the Russian Revolution," *American Slavic and East European Review*, XXII:2 (April 1961).

10. Alexander Solzhenitsyn, *Bodalsya telenok s dubom: Ocherki literaturnoi zhizni* (Paris: YMCA Press, 1975); *The Oak and the Calf: Sketches of Literary Life in the Soviet Union* (New York: Harper and Row, 1980), p. 10.

11. *Biulleten' Oppozitsii*, no. 3–4 (September 1929), no. 6 (October 1929), no. 17–18 (November–December 1930); excerpts translated in Robert V. Daniels, *A Documentary History of Communism*, (Hanover, N.H.: University Press of New England, 1984), vol. I, pp. 222–224.

12. See Jan Waclaw Makhaiski, *Le socialisme des intellectuels*, edited by Alexandre Skirda (Paris: Editions du Seuil, 1979).

13. James Burnham, *The Managerial Revolution* (New York: John Day, 1941); Bruno Rizzi, *La bureaucratization du monde* (Paris, 1939. *The Bureaucratization of the World*, New York: The Free Press, 1985); Milovan Djilas, *The New Class* (New York: Praeger, 1957).

14. See, *inter alia*, George Konrad and Ivan Szelenyi, *The Intellectuals on the Road to Class Power* (New York: Harcourt, Brace & Jovanovich, 1979).

15. Antonio Carlo, "The Socio-Economic Nature of the USSR," *Telos*, no. 21 (fall 1974), p. 45.

16. Luca Meldolesi, *L'utopia realmente esistente: Marx e Saint Simon* (The Really Existing Utopia: Marx and Saint-Simon, Rome and Bari: Laterza, 1982).

17. Svetozar Stojanović, "Marxism and Democracy: The Ruling Class or the Dominant Class?" *Praxis International*, I:2 (July 1981).

18. David Joravsky, "Political Authorities and the Learned Estate," *Survey*, XXIII:1 (winter 1977/78), pp. 36–37.

19. Interview with A. I. Volodin, *Pravda*, March 10, 1987.

20. Marshall S. Shatz, *Soviet Dissent in Historical Perspective* (Cambridge, England: Cambridge University Press, 1980), p. 11.

21. Vittorio Strada, "Politica e cultura nell'URSS" (Politics and Culture in the USSR), in Sergio Bertolissi, ed., *Momenti e problemi della storia dell'URSS* (Forces and Problems in the History of the USSR, Rome: Riuniti, 1978), p. 163.

22. Ibid., p. 166.

23. *Ogonyok*, July 11, 1987.

24. Sergio Bertolissi, Fabio Bettanin, and Lapo Sestan, "Stalinismo e continuità nello sviluppo storico sovietico" (Stalinism and Continuity in Soviet Historical Development), *Momenti e problemi della storia dell'URSS*, p. 177.

25. The theme of support of Stalinism by the new petty-bourgeoisie or *meshchanstvo* is argued from quite different perspectives by Roy Medvedev, *On Stalin and Stalinism* (New York: Oxford University Press, 1979), and by the literary historian Vera Dunham, *In Stalin's Time: Middle Class Values in Soviet Fiction* (Cambridge, England: Cambridge University Press, 1976).

26. David K. Shipler, *Russia: Broken Idols, Solemn Dreams* (New York: Times Books, 1983), p. 344.

27. Giuseppe Boffa, *Storia dell'Unione Sovietica* (History of the Soviet Union, Milan: Mondadori, 1979), vol. II, p. 514.

28. Isabelle Esmein, "Aperçu chronologique sur les relations entre les intellectuels et le parti en URSS avant et après la chute de N. Khrouchtchev" (Chronological View of the Relations Between the Intellectuals and the Party in the USSR Before and After the Fall of N. Khrushchev), *Cahiers du Monde Russe et Sovietique*, VI:4 (October–December 1965), p. 561.

29. Ilya Erenburg, *Ottepel'*, Part I, *Znamya*, May 1954; *The Thaw* (Chicago: Regnery, 1955).

30. *Pravda*, October 6, 1952; Leo Gruliow, ed., *Current Soviet Policies* (New York: Praeger, 1953), p. 115.

31. Robert Conquest, *Power and Policy in the USSR: The Study of Soviet Dynastics* (London: Macmillan, 1961), p. 248.

32. See Edith R. Frankel, *Novy Mir: A Case Study in the Politics of Literature, 1952–1958* (Cambridge, England: Cambridge University Press, 1981), p. 67.

33. George Gibian, *Interval of Freedom: Soviet Literature during the Thaw, 1954–1957* (Minneapolis: University of Minnesota Press, 1960), p. 9.

34. Ibid., pp. 11–12.

35. Bukharin–Kamenev talk, July 11, 1928, notes by Kamenev, Trotsky Archive, Harvard University, T 1897; translated in Daniels, *A Documentary History of Communism*, vol. I, p. 207.

36. *Pravda*, February 15, 1956; Leo Gruliow, ed., *Current Soviet Policies*, vol. II (New York: Praeger, 1957), p. 61.

37. Ibid., p. 86.

38. Ibid., p. 118.

39. Frankel, *Novy Mir*, p. 78.

40. Solzhenitsyn, *The Oak and the Calf*, p. 9.

41. B. A. Nazarov and O. V. Gridneva, "On the Problem of the Lag in Drama and Theater," *Voprosy filosofii*, no. 5, 1956.

42. See Gibian, *Interval of Freedom*, pp. 13–15.

43. Giuseppe Boffa, *Inside the Khrushchev Era* (New York: Marzani and Munsell, 1959), p. 189.

44. A. Kron, "A Writer's Notes," *Literaturnaya Moskva*, no. 2, 1956, quoted in Gibian, *Interval of Freedom*, p. 15.

45. V. D. Dudintsev, *Ne Khlebom edinym*, serialized in *Novyi Mir*, nos. 8–10 (August–October), 1956; *Not By Bread Alone* (New York: Dutton, 1957).

46. "On Overcoming the Cult of the Individual and Its Consequences," *Pravda*, July 2, 1956; *Current Soviet Policies*, II, pp. 221–227. Cf. Roy and Zhores Medvedev, *Khrushchev: The Years in Power* (New York: Columbia University Press, 1976), p. 71; Boffa, *Storia dell'Unione Sovietica*, vol. II, pp. 510–511.

47. Conquest, *Power and Policy*, p. 293.

48. Abraham Rothberg, *The Heirs of Stalin: Dissidence and the Soviet Regime, 1953–1970* (Ithaca, N.Y.: Cornell University Press, 1972), pp. 30–31.

49. *Sovetskaya Kultura*, November 20, 1956.

50. *Partiinaya Zhizn'*, no. 24, 1956, pp. 60–64, cited in Frankel, *Novy Mir*, p. 101.

51. Esmein, "Aperçu chronologique," p. 569.

52. "For Leninist Adherence to Principle in Questions of Literature and the Arts," *Kommunist*, no. 10, 1957.

53. N. S. Khrushchev, "For Close Tie between Literature and Art and the Life of the People," *Pravda*, August 28, 1957; Thomas P. Whitney, ed., *Khrushchev Speaks* (Ann Arbor: University of Michigan Press, 1963), p. 285. This article was an amalgam of Khrushchev's speeches of May and July.

54. "For Leninist Adherence to Principle," p. 6.

55. Discussion with Ivan Anisimov and Ignazio Silone, *Encounter*, VIII:6 (June 1957), p. 65.

56. *Pravda*, February 2, 1959; Leo Gruliow, ed., *Current Soviet Policies*, vol. III (New York: Columbia University Press, 1960), pp. 133–134.

57. *Pravda*, May 24, 1959; Ronald Hingley, "The Soviet Writers' Congress, *Soviet Survey*, July–September, 1959, pp. 14–15.

58. Peter Benno, "The Political Aspect," in Max Hayward and Edward L. Crowley, eds., *Soviet Literature in the Sixties* (London: Methuen, 1965), p. 181.

59. *Literaturnaya Gazeta*, September 19, 1961.

60. "Odin den' Ivana Denisovicha," *Novyi Mir*, November 1962; *One Day in the Life of Ivan Denisovich* (New York: Dutton, 1963).

61. Rothberg, *The Heirs of Stalin*, pp. 56–57, 394–395.

62. *Ogonyok*, February 9, 1987.

63. Boffa, *Storia dell'Unione Sovietica*, vol. II, pp. 603–604.

64. See Sheila Fitzpatrick, "Stalin and the Making of the New Elite, 1928–1939," *Slavic Review*, XXXVIII:3 (September 1979); Michal Reiman, "Spontaneity and Planning in the Plebian Revolution," in Ralph Carter Elwood, ed., *Reconsiderations on the Russian Revolution* (Cambridge, Mass.: Slavica, 1976).

65. Recounted by a Western diplomat to Michel Tatu, *Power in the Kremlin from Khrushchev to Kosygin* (New York: Viking, 1969), p. 306.

66. Robert V. Daniels, *Russia—The Roots of Confrontation* (Cambridge, Mass.: Harvard University Press, 1985), pp. 188–189. See also Tatu, *Power in the Kremlin*, ch. 2.

67. Priscilla Johnson, *Khrushchev and the Arts: The Politics of Soviet Culture, 1962–1964* (Cambridge, Mass.: MIT Press, 1965), pp. 7–9. The purported transcript of Khrushchev's remarks first appeared in *Encounter*, XXVIII:4 (April 1963), pp.

102–103. Johnson, seconded by Rothberg (*The Heirs of Stalin*, pp. 62, 396 n. 3), expresses the suspicion that the Manezh affair was either a conservative provocation or a stage-managed maneuver by Khrushchev himself.

68. *Pravda*, March 10, 1963.

69. Solzhenitsyn, *The Oak and the Calf*, pp. 70–72.

5

The Political System and
the Generational Revolution

It remains a fact of Soviet political life in the 1980s as it was in the 1960s that the realization of reform depends on the frame of mind of the bureaucratic leadership. For two decades following the overthrow of Khrushchev this meant reaction and immobilism and national frustration seemingly without end. Yet changes were taking place in the party hierarchy, signalled finally by the triple succession to Brezhnev and the leadership renovation registered by the Twenty-Seventh Party Congress of February and March, 1986, that opened the road to more enduring reform and made possible a new relationship between the politically ruling bureaucracy and the ever more socially dominant intelligentsia. The Twenty-Seventh Congress in fact climaxed one of the most decisive transition periods in Soviet political history. Not only had the country gone through an unprecedented series of leadership changes, with the successive deaths of three national chiefs in less than two and a half years; the replacement of a whole generation in the bureaucratic elite was consummated as well.

To be sure, these experiences did not constitute a crisis for the Soviet political system as such. Indeed, the continuity of the real mechanisms of power in the Communist Party, dating at least from the death of Stalin and in some respects from the 1920s, was powerfully reaffirmed by the events of 1982–1986.

This persistence of the Communist power structure through years of great turmoil among the personalities who managed it prompts a series of questions about the nature of political power in the Soviet system. Where is real power located and on what basis does it rest? How is power mobilized and transferred? What difference does the succession from one generation to another make, as the experience of Stalinism recedes into the past?

These questions are made no easier by the vast gulf between formal and actual structures of power in the Soviet Union, and the difficulty

75

of accurately determining what is real behind the fog of ideological rhetoric. It is easy to go to the opposite extreme from Soviet constitutional pretenses and embrace the simplistic totalitarian model wherein all power emanates from the man at the top. And it is almost as easy, as time erodes this image, to overcompensate for the overcompensation and to underrate the elements of totalitarianism still operating in the system.

As T. H. Rigby argues, the Soviet political system has become basically oligarchic rather than personalist since 1953.[1] Within this framework, at the upper levels of the Soviet hierarchy a form of real politics does take place, contrary to the totalitarian model.[2] However, as at the Muscovite Court, politics in this realm is masked and insulated by the compulsion to suppress open controversy and present the public appearance of monolithic unity. Soviet elite politics, involving bureaucratic infighting, special interest pressure, deals and coalitions, as well as actual voting at the top level, is more akin to the politics within large subnational organizations in Western society (government bureaucracies, corporations, universities, churches) than to the electoral politics that still constitutes the broadest, integrating form of politics in democratic countries. At the same time we must recognize the continuing influence of Russian political culture and its popular assumptions and expectations, non-verbal or at least non-public, about how government should be conducted. This source helps account for some of the distinctive forms and processes of bureaucratic life that lie behind the published record.[3]

The aim of this chapter is to bring all of these questions down to empirical earth by investigating the political behavior of that distinctive Soviet elite population that is institutionalized in the Central Committee of the Party, together with the "Candidate" or alternate members of the Central Committee and the members of the Central Auditing Commission (CAC—really a category of honorable mention just beneath the Central Committee). I will undertake to describe, as far as known data and reasonable inference permit, changes in the demography of this body of power-wielders and the structure of political relationships among them.

The inquiry begins with an account of the remarkably enduring generation of leaders who dominated Soviet political life from the purges of the 1930s down to the 1980s. Next comes an examination of the structure of the Soviet elite in terms of membership in the top party organs and the job-slot system of status and representation. This is followed by an analysis of the transfer and accumulation of leadership power through what I term the "circular flow of power." I follow these processes as they operated in the Brezhnev era and during the generational transition of the triple succession. Finally I shall attempt to appraise the consolidation of a new leadership generation as it was manifested at the Twenty-Seventh Congress.

1. The Era of the Post-Purge Generation

Compared with the political and social turmoil that extended with only short periods of respite from World War I to the purges, the Soviet Union has experienced since the late 1930s an extraordinary history of institutional stability and continuity. Even the staggering challenges of World War II and its aftermath disturbed the emergent structure of Stalinist government and society relatively little. Reflecting this continuity and contributing to it was a remarkable generational phenomenon in the Soviet leadership—the perpetuation in power of one distinctive age cohort, which inherited its position as the beneficiary of the purges, and then as a group grew old in office until the laws of biology caught up with it in the 1980s.[4]

A little-recognized fact about Stalin's purges, specifically the *Yezhovshchina* or secret mass purge of Stalinist officials, was its age-based cut-off. Apart from the Politburo and a few other Stalin cronies,[5] virtually everyone in Soviet public life who was over the age of 37 in 1937 was eliminated from the scene. This criterion is revealed in the otherwise inexplicable observation that hardly anyone was available afterwards to serve in the Soviet leadership at the Central Committee level who had been born before 1900. (For the military, the cut-off birth year was 1897.) Among the 125 full members of Stalin's last Central Committee in 1952, only 27 men or 22% (mostly actual or former Politburo members, military men, or theoreticians) had been born before 1900; the median age was only 49.6.[6] On the other hand, of all those members whose birth year is known there were only seven born after 1912 and thus under age 40 in 1952.

This extraordinary generational compression in the postwar leadership underscores how, to fill the shoes of purge victims up and down the bureaucracy, Stalin had turned to his younger cadres. Their rise in the post-purge vacuum was meteoric. To take one well-known example, Aleksei Kosygin, born in 1904, ascended from factory manager to deputy prime minister in just two years. Leonid Brezhnev, born in 1906, rose from industrial engineer to deputy party boss of a province in the same length of time.

Once they had filled all the empty slots in the bureaucracy, normal life expectancy assured the youthful purge beneficiaries of an extraordinary tenure of office. Furthermore, the leaders of this cohort made sure that replacements, when they had to be made, were nearly of the same age group. Naturally, age mates more readily met the appointment criteria cited by John Miller, of familiarity and dependability, when there was no physical need to go to younger people.[7] In consequence, one generation, marked by distinctive qualities in its selection and experience, dominated the Soviet political scene for nearly half a century.

The post-purge generation of the "class of '38" shared a unique set of characteristics. They were defined, first of all, by the age cut-off of the purges. Typically they were the fruit of Stalin's efforts in the early 1930s to recruit bright, tough young men as potential candidates for the party and state officialdom. They were the *vydvizhentsy* ("promotees") described by Sheila Fitzpatrick—sons of peasants or grandsons of peasants, who had been put through crash courses in engineering and agitprop to prepare them for higher responsibilities.[8] As a type the *vydvizhentsy* seem to have been authoritarian, anti-intellectual, xenophobic, and anti-Semitic. They evidently embodied what Edward Keenan has termed the "fusion" of the self-protective political culture of the Russian village and the quasi-paranoid but pragmatic political culture of the Russian bureaucracy.[9] Finally, they were indelibly molded in their formative careers by the successive traumas of the purges and the Second World War, so that they were "survivors" in every sense of the word.

Thanks to their selectivity based on youth, the post-purge leadership had the potential for extraordinary longevity in office as a generation. This demographic fact was the basis for the remarkable stability and slow turnover manifested in the Soviet leadership at the level of Central Committee membership after the disruptions of the immediate post-Stalin years had passed. Table 1 indicates the rate of holdovers in the successive five-year intervals from one Central Committee to the next, from 1952–1956 to 1981–1986. These figures demonstrate the very high degree of continuity in the Soviet bureaucratic elite from 1961 to 1981, particularly when the count includes members who were previously at any one of the three prestige ranks. The abnormally high turnover of 1961, at a time when Khrushchev had presumably consolidated his power, is a problem that I will address later on.

Inevitably, the low rate of turnover meant that the leadership body as a whole was aging steadily, as renovation failed to keep pace with the passage of time. Table 2 shows how the median age of the Central Committee rose during this era at the rate of one year of age for each two years of elapsed time. Renovation did not even occur as fast as the turnover rate might have allowed; age was not a decisive criterion for retirement at each congress, and replacements tended to be made with people from the Candidate and CAC ranks who were not much younger than the aging holdovers. As a result, the median people of 1952 and 1981, over a span of nearly three decades, were born only 14 years apart, in 1904 and 1918 respectively, biologically within the same

TABLE 1
Turnover in the Central Committee Elite

	1956	1961	1966	1971	1976	1981	1986
CC members	133	175	195	241	287	319	307
Number held over from							
previous CC	79	66	139	149	201	230	172
Percent	59.4	37.7	71.3	68.1	70.0	72.1	56.0
Number held over or							
promoted from							
Candidate or CAC	94	97	170	195	251	278	215
Percent	70.7	55.4	87.2	80.9	87.5	87.1	70.0
Candidate members	122	155	165	155	139	151	170
CAC members	63	65	79	81	85	75	83
All ranks	318	395	439	477	511	545	560
Number of all ranks							
held over	174	158	277	313	369	392	304
Percent	54.7	40.0	63.1	65.6	72.2	71.9	54.3

TABLE 2
Aging of the Central Committee

Central Committee	1952	1956	1961	1966	1971	1976	1981	1986
All full members	125	133	175	195	241	287	319	307
Median birth year	1904	1906	1908	1910	1913	1915/16	1918	1924
Median age	48	50	53	56	58	60.5	63	62
Holdover members		79	66	139	149	201	230	172
Median birth year		1903	1906	1909	1911	1914	1916	1923
Median age		53	55	57	60	62	65	63
New and promoted								
members		54	109	56	92	86	89	135
Median birth year		1908	1910	1912	1918	1921	1923	1930
Median age		48	51	54	53	55	58	56
Members retained								
through 1981	12	19	51	82	153	230		
Median birth year	1906/7	1905	1911	1911	1914	1917		
Median age in 1981	74.5	76	70	70	67	65		

generation as its leading and trailing edges, so to speak. Significantly, the median members of 1981 had still come out of the same basic experience as Stalin's last Central Committee of 1952—the purge of their elders as they themselves were moving from the Komsomol to the party; service in World War II; and promotion into the power-wielding class of the nomenklatura while Stalin was still living and tyrannizing the country.

The natural consequences of the perpetuation of this aging generation of leadership have been widely recognized in the literature on Soviet politics. The post-purge officialdom was, by virtue of its origin, experience, and ossification in office, conservative and self-protective in its reflexes. It resisted or sabotaged innovation and clung to sterile bureaucratic methods and ideological formulas in the face of the new problems and potential of a modern society. To be sure, new blood was not entirely excluded from the leadership, and the steady expansion in the membership of the Central Committee made it possible to bring in some younger and better educated people without winnowing the older cohorts at the same rate. Nevertheless, most of the new blood was, as the age data show, progressively older and more tired when it too reached the level of Central Committee membership. It was only a matter of time when illness, incapacity, and death would break the grip of the post-purge generation. This is precisely what occurred between the death of Brezhnev and the Twenty-Seventh Congress.

2. The Structure of the Party Elite

The study of Soviet elite politics and of the structures and practices that shape that mysterious realm of human behavior is facilitated by the actual way in which the organization of the Communist Party defines its leadership elite. This is no more and no less than the Central Committee of the party, together with its Candidate members and the members of the CAC. The Central Committee elite thus defined is a natural unit for the study of the Soviet leadership, not simply because it is the party's statutory policy-making body, but because it is made up to represent the top personnel in all sectors of Soviet society, according to their imputed importance. This representation is governed by the set of unwritten laws or "conventions" that I have already alluded to.

Membership in the Central Committee elite at any one of the three ranks—full member, Candidate member, or CAC—is not simply a reflection of personal eminence, nor is it a mere honorific (save for the small group that I call "mass representatives," the token workers, dairy maids, and factory directors who are picked to represent various social categories of the population at large[10]). Systematic analysis of the composition of the Central Committee shows that ever since the late 1920s, membership has been accorded almost exclusively on the basis of the tenure of high bureaucratic office in the party apparatus, the civil government, and the military, with small numbers allocated to the top people in the trade unions, diplomacy, and cultural and scientific work.[11] With few exceptions, allocation of seats at the three ranks to the various functional areas as well as to the geographical divisions of the country is arranged in close proportion to the importance of the given function or region. Individuals are automatically elevated to the Central Committee at the next party congress after their appointment to a job carrying Central Committee rank (and reportedly attend meetings from the time of the entitling appointment[12]). Conversely, individuals who are removed or retired from one of these elite positions, and not assigned to another, are almost always dropped from the Central Committee at the next congress (although they might still attend meetings until that time).

The fine lines of functional and regional status in the make-up of the Central Committee underscore a compulsion about rank and precedence that appears to be deeply embedded in Russian political culture. They reveal, if more evidence were needed, that the slate of Central Committee members voted in unanimously at each party congress must have been carefully prepared by the central authorities to reflect the appointments and removals effected since the previous congress, and to maintain the required balance and rank of representation for all the functional hierarchies and geographical areas simultaneously.

The Central Committee elected at the Twenty-sixth Congress in 1981, the last under Brezhnev, reflected the long-standing order of precedence in the allocation of seats. Taking all three ranks together, a total of 545 individuals, there were 211 (62%) from the full-time party apparatus; 179 (33%) from the civil government (central and union republics); 40 (7%) from the military; 6 from the police agencies; 21 ambassadors (usually former party officials); 11 trade union officials; 22 cultural and scientific officials; 4 heads of miscellaneous "social organizations," and 51 (9%) mass representatives. Geographically the party and government categories broke down as shown in Table 3, with a clear ranking in representation according to the importance of the republic, and a consistent precedence of party representation over governmental.

The new list established by the Twenty-Seventh Congress, despite a surge in the rate of membership turnover, deviated hardly at all from the representative proportions observed in 1981. Table 4 demonstrates the degree of constancy in the allocation of full member seats, though there was a significant reduction in governmental jobs with Central Committee rank and a distinct increase in the category of mass representatives (practically all accounted for by adding women from the RSFSR). In short, the job-slot system of status and representation was faithfully observed by the new Gorbachev leadership, whatever its other commitments to reform.

A particularly revealing illustration of the Soviet leadership's unavowed status consciousness and the steps used to implement it is the allocation of Central Committee seats to the various union republics. This involves a simultaneous calculation of the relative status of different functional

TABLE 3

Party and Government Representation in the Central Committee Elite, by Geographical Area (Members, Candidate Members, and Central Auditing Commission, 1981 and 1986)

	Party		Government	
	1981	1986	1981	1986
Central	63	49	123	124
RSFSR	80	87	21	18
Union Republics	68	77	35	35
Ukraine	24	25	6	7
Kazakhstan	14	16	3	3
Uzbekistan	6	6	3	3
Belorussia	5	7	3	4
Georgia	2	2	2	1[a]
Azerbaidzhan	2	2	2	2
Latvia	2	2	2	2
Kirgizia	2	2	2	1[a]
Moldavia	2	2	2	2
Lithuania	2	2	2	2
Tadzhikistan	2	2	2	2
Armenia	2	2	2	2
Turkmenia	2	2	2	2
Estonia	2	2	2	2

[a]See note b, Table 5.

hierarchies, particular jobs, and individual republics, and the assignment of seats accordingly, both in number and by rank. A status matrix, as shown in Table 5, can be constructed to demonstrate the unspoken rules that operate, now as in the past, to govern the distribution of seats and ranks. The regularity of the patterns generated by these rules is persuasive evidence of the fine attention given at the party center to the prestige implications of all appointments.

In a more visible though less firmly established way the job-slot principle of status is carried up into the Politburo itself. The pattern and its consistency are clear if Politburo positions are arranged for each congress year according to the incumbents' functions. Table 6 shows the close relationship of Politburo membership to high party and government office, as well as the striking stability in the positions represented, particularly when Politburo Candidate status is considered along with full membership. The remarkable continuity of individual incumbents in jobs of Politburo rank during the Brezhnev era stands out as well. There are very few anomalies: the brief heyday of the chairmanship of the Trade Unions, when that office was utilized to shunt Alexander Shelepin away from a bid for power; and the unusual status of the Ministry of Culture during the incumbency of ex-Secretariat member

TABLE 4
Allocation of Full Central Committee Seats, 1981 and 1986 (women in brackets)

	1981			1986			Change	Percent Change in Share
	Number	Percent		Number	Percent			
Total	319	100	[8]	307	100	[12]		
Party Apparatus	140	43.9	[1]	135	44.0	[1]	-5	+0.2
Central	33	10.3		33	10.7	[1]		
RSFSR	66	20.7	[1]	63	20.5		-3	
Union Republics	41	12.9		39	12.7		-2	
Government	101	31.7	[2]	84	27.4	[1]	-17	-13.6
Central	81	25.4		69	22.5		-12	
RSFSR	10	3.1	[2]	9	2.9	[1]	-1	
Union Republics	10	3.1		6	2.0		-4	
Other	78		[5]	88		[10]	+10	
Military	23	7.2		24	7.8		+1	+5.6
Police	5	1.6		5	1.6			
Trade Unions	5	1.6	[1]	4	1.3		-1	
Diplomats	13	4.1		11	3.6		-2	
Culture and Science	11	3.4		10	3.3		-1	
Social Organizations	2	0.6	[2]	3	1.0	[2]	-1	
Mass Representatives	19	6.0	[2]	27	8.8	[8]	+8	+46.7
RSFSR	15		[2]	22		[8]	+7	
Union Republics	4			5			+1	
Retired Dignitaries				4	1.3		+4	

Pyotr Demichev. The precedence of the party apparatus over the government and the scaled representation of union republics, so clear in the apportionment of the Central Committee, are replicated in miniature in the Politburo.[13]

Comparison of the 1986 Politburo with earlier years shows that despite the sweeping change in leading personnel that took place during the transition after Brezhnev, Gorbachev has continued to observe the established rules in awarding rank in the Politburo as well as in the Central Committee. Nowhere has he deviated from precedent, except to downgrade the non-Slavic republics and to bring in the new head of Gosplan (a position not represented since the 1950s). Expectations of Politburo status for the country's top jobs are now so firm that the leader can do little more than marginally adjust the ranks accorded them.

The tradition of making up the Politburo as well as the Central Committee on the basis of the status of particular individuals' jobs is a conservative and stabilizing element in Soviet politics. It is another circumstance contributing to the long political lives of the post-purge generation. Within the terms of the job-slot tradition, no change in the

Central Committee or the Politburo is possible without removing the given individual from the bureaucratic command that conferred the particular rank on him in the first place. To accomplish a sudden overturn in the leadership bodies would require a corresponding sweep of the upper bureaucratic hierarchy. Short of a Stalin-style reign of terror, such a campaign would quickly arouse a defensive coalition among the apparatchiki and put the leader's power in jeopardy. The less risky alternative is simply to wait for targeted individuals to die or fall into decrepitude. However, given the age composition of the post-purge generation, this made any wholesale housecleaning impossible before the late 1970s.

The long tenure of a stable and aging leadership generation in the CPSU was physically possible to begin with because the traumatic renovation of the party brought about by Stalin's purges had installed a uniformly youthful cadre of Communist leaders. But barring a new purge, the party's institutionalized practices of appointment to high bureaucratic positions constituted a major obstacle to further rapid renovation until the post-purge generation began to reach retirement age a third of a century after its advent in power. Even the quasi-purge of 1956–1961, reflected in the unusual level of Central Committee turnover in 1961, failed to undercut the ruling generation, as incumbents of high-status positions were replaced by people of virtually the same age cohort. Here is the explanation, based on a combination of institutional and demographic factors, for the strong continuity in the Soviet leadership during the Brezhnev era.

By the same token, the inevitable demographic revolution represented by the passing of the post-purge generation created unusual possibilities instead of unusual resistance for personnel changes. Thereby Brezhnev's successors, above all Gorbachev, could seize the opportunity for new appointments in the party and governmental machinery, and reshape the composition of the Central Committee as their new appointees were promoted to it. This opportunity was the key to the process of creating a new basis of personal leadership and policy.

3. Succession Politics and the Circular Flow of Power

Real political power in the Soviet system, as outside observers almost universally recognize, is not constitutional but informal. The power of a Soviet leader may be likened to the power of an old-fashioned American party boss, except that the challenge of competing parties or the constraints of a federal system are excluded. Neither the identity of the leader nor the degree of his personal power are determined by rule or

TABLE 5
Status Matrices: Central Committee Representation of Union Republics, 1981 and 1986

Republic	First Secretary	Second Secretary	Prime Minister	Chrm Presid. Sup. Sov.	1st Dep. Prime Min.	Other Seats
1981						
Ukraine	PB	CC	CC	CC	CC, Cand.	CC (14) Cand. (8) CAC (4)
Kazakhstan	PB	CC	CC	CC	CAC	CC (6) Cand. (5) CAC (2)
Belorussia	Cand.PB	CC	CC	CC	CAC	CC,Cand.(2)
Uzbekistan	Cand.PB	CC	CC	CC	CAC	CC,Cand.(2) CAC
Georgia	Cand.PB	CC	Cand.	CAC		
Azerbaidzhan	Cand.PB	Cand.	Cand.	CAC		
Latvia	CC	Cand.	Cand.	CAC		
Kirgizia	CC	Cand.	Cand.	CAC		
Moldavia	CC	Cand.	CAC	Cand.		
Lithuania	CC	Cand.	CAC	Cand.		
Tadzhikistan	CC	Cand.	CAC	Cand.		
Armenia	CC	Cand.	CAC	Cand.		
Estonia	CC	Cand.	Cand.	CC[a]		
Turkmenia	CC	Cand.	CAC	Cand.		
1986						
Ukraine	PB	CC	CC	CC	CC, Cand.	CC (13) Cand.(10) CAC (3)
Kazakhstan	PB	CC	CC	Cand.	CAC	CC (3) Cand. (7) CAC (4)
Belorussia	Cand.PB	CC	CC	CC	CC	CC (2) Cand. (3)
Uzbekistan	CC	CC	Cand.	CC	CAC	Cand. (4)
Georgia	CC	CC	—[b]	CAC		
Azerbaidzhan	CC	Cand.	Cand.	CAC		
Latvia	CC	Cand.	Cand.	CAC		
Kirgizia	CC	Cand.	—[b]	CAC		
Moldavia	CC	Cand.	Cand.	CAC		
Lithuania	CC	Cand.	Cand.	CAC		
Tadzhikistan	CC	Cand.	Cand.	CAC		
Armenia	CC	Cand.	Cand.	CAC		
Estonia	CC	Cand.	Cand.	CAC		
Turkmenia	CC	Cand.	CAC	Cand.		

[a]Anomaly: The former Estonia First Secretary Kebin was allowed to keep his CC seat after being shunted to CPSS.
[b]Evidently vacant, filled after congress.

TABLE 6
Functional Representation in the Politburo, 1966–1986 (candidate status in parentheses)

Position	1966	1971	1976	1981	1986
Party Apparatus					
General Secretary	Brezhnev	Brezhnev	Brezhnev	Brezhnev	Gorbachev
Secretariat	Suslov	Suslov	Suslov	Suslov	Ligachev
	Kirilenko	Kirilenko	Kirilenko	Kirilenko	Zaikov
	Shelepin	Kulakov	Ustinov[a]	Chernenko	(Dolgikh)
	(Ustinov)	(Ustinov)	(Ponomarev)	Gorbachev	
	(Demichev)	(Demichev)		(Ponomarev)	
Chrm. Party Control Comm.	Pelshe	Pelshe	Pelshe	Pelshe	Solomentsev
1st Sec. Ukraine	Shelest	Shelest	Shcherbitsky	Shcherbitsky	Shcherbitsky
1st Sec. Kazakhstan	(Kunaev)	Kunaev	Kunaev	Kunaev	Kunaev
1st Sec. Moscow City		Grishin	Grishin	Grishin	(Eltsin)
1st Sec. Leningrad Province			Romanov	Romanov	(Soloviev)
1st Sec. Belorussia	(Masherov)	(Masherov)	(Masherov)	(Kiselev)	(Slyunkov)
1st Sec. Uzbekistan	(Rashidov)	(Rashidov)	(Rashidov)	(Rashidov)	
1st Sec. Georgia	(Mzhavanadze)	(Mzhavanadze)		(Shevardnadze)	
1st Sec. Azerbaidzhan			(Aliev)	(Aliev)	

Government					
Prime Minister	Kosygin	Kosygin	Kosygin	Tikhonov	Ryzhkov
Chrm. Presidium Supreme Soviet	Podgorny	Podgorny	Podgorny	(Kuznetsov)[b]	Gromyko
1st Dep. Prime Min.	Mazurov Polianksy	Mazurov Polianksy	Mazurov		Aliev
Prime Min. RSFSR	Voronov	Voronov	(Solomentsev)	(Solomentsev)	Vorotnikov
Prime Min. Ukraine	(Shcherbitsky)	Shcherbitsky			
Min. of Defense			Grechko[a]	Ustinov	(Sokolov)
Min. of Foreign Affairs		(Andropov)	Gromyko	Gromyko	Shevardnadze
Chairman KGB			Andropov	Andropov	Chebrikov
Chairman Gosplan					(Talyzin)
Min. of Culture			(Demichev)	(Demichev)	(Demichev)[b]
Other					
Chrm. Trade Unions	(Grishin)	Shelepin			
Total Members	11 (8)	15 (6)	15 (6)	14 (8)	12 (7)

[a]Grechko died immediately after the 25th Congress and was replaced by Ustinov.
[b]Kuznetsov was First Vice-Chairman of the Presidium of the Supreme Soviet when Brezhnev held the title of Chairman. Demichev was given this position shortly after the 27th Congress.

by genuine popular mandate. Power is won or accumulated by leaders through oligarchic infighting and the manipulation of the constitutional structures of the party and the government to assure the bureaucratic base for their authority. In other words, power in the Soviet system follows what may be imagined as a circular path, particularly evident at moments of the transfer of power, that runs from the General Secretary down the hierarchy of secretaries by way of his power of bureaucratic appointment, over to the nominally representative structure of the party organization, with its several tiers of committees, and up to the Party Congress and the Central Committee that confirm the authority of the man in charge, and so on around again, ever more tightly.[14]

The origin of this circle of bureaucratic control over a formally democratic organization is commonly attributed to Lenin's doctrine of democratic centralism. Oddly enough, when Lenin originally put forth the term in 1906, he was defending himself against the Menshevik faction and arguing to allow the democratic element of free criticism in arriving at party decisions, within the context of united action.[15] It was neither doctrine nor the events of the Bolshevik Revolution, but the life-or-death struggle of the Russian Civil War that put an absolute premium on the centralist element in democratic centralism. The original formula was preserved, and continues now to be used, mainly as a textual justification for the exclusion of any opposition voice.[16]

By 1919 the military exigencies of survival had made it imperative for the revolutionary government to forge a direct chain of authority that could overcome the spontaneous localism of the soviets of 1917 and 1918.[17] The Eighth Party Congress took the crucial step with its famous resolution "On The Organizational Question," to affirm the principle of central control over local party organizations, as well as to formalize the party leadership in the Politburo, the Orgburo, and the Secretariat. Simultaneously, in the provinces, the regional and local party secretaries emerged as the key power figures, dominating the nominally deliberative processes in the party organizations and the local soviets.[18] The secretaries were (as they still are) theoretically elected by their respective party committees, but in practice the central authority increasingly used its power of "recommendation," i.e. *de facto* transfer and appointment of local officials backed up by the sanctions of party discipline.

By 1920–1921, central pressure was being exerted to remove members of the various opposition factions from local positions of power in the party. Shortly after the Red Army reoccupied the Ukraine in the spring of 1920, the entire Ukrainian Communist Central Committee membership was ordered out of the region, even though the Ukraine at the time was technically an independent Communist state. The same thing happened in 1922 to the party committee of the Samara (now Kuibyshev) province, the only place where the Workers' Opposition had won province-wide control.[19]

After 1921 it remained only for the practice of central control through *de facto* appointment of party secretaries to be made systematic. This was Stalin's decisive work, which he accomplished in the course of his rise to personal power that rested above all on that achievement. Stalin gained *de facto* control of the party Secretariat after the shake-up of 1921 removed the Trotskyists who had run it since 1919. The following year he won the organizational leadership *de jure* with his installation in the newly created office of General Secretary. Immediately he went to work, using the new practice of appointment, to put his own men in place as local secretaries. They in turn used their local power to control the election of delegates to the next party congress, the Twelfth, held in April 1923.

With Lenin ill and effectively out of the picture by this time, Stalin seized upon the then popular notion of reforming the party by expanding the Central Committee with "ordinary workers." The bulk of these turned out in practice to be Stalin's newly designated provincial leaders, rewarded by inclusion on the official slate for membership or Candidate membership.[20] In this way Stalin began building up the network of boss-client relationships that has characterized Soviet politics ever since, often creating clients simply by the favor of appointment (though this process was not altogether foolproof).

Originally Central Committee members were voted on individually by the congress delegates, but in 1921 Lenin started the practice of proposing an official slate, and from 1922 on individual vote totals were suppressed. In 1923, without attacking the Old Bolsheviks in the Central Committee head-on, Stalin combined an expansion proposal (from 27 to 40 members) and the slate-making technique to control the selection of 16 new and replacement members, as well as 14 new Candidate members. He continued the same process of expanding the Central Committee and filling vacancies with slates of his own appointees until he achieved complete domination of the body in 1927.

Since Stalin's basis for choosing people for the Central Committee was his own appointments to the leading provincial posts in the party (as well as a number of People's Commissars in the central government), the Central Committee began at this early date to acquire its present compositional character as an assemblage of top bureaucratic office holders rather than a group of "revolutionary notables."[21] The new process of selection made the criteria for membership in the formal Soviet leadership remarkably similar to the prerevolutionary Council of State or the Petrine Table of Ranks—just one way in which the organization and operation of the Soviet regime were taking on the color of Tsarist bureaucratic practice.

By capitalizing on the practicality and acceptability of bureaucratizing the party from top to bottom, Stalin rapidly built the personal power base from which he would eventually challenge and destroy his rivals among the revolutionary notables. With his hold over the local party organizations through the appointment power, his control through his local clients over the party's electoral processes, and his ability to dictate access to the Central Committee, he could completely manipulate the machinery that confirmed his own power as General Secretary. It was only a matter of time for him to complete the power circuit by eliminating the luminaries who had shared authority with him in the Politburo, and replacing them with his own creatures. Trotsky, Zinoviev, and Kamenev were disgraced and expelled from the party prior to the Fifteenth Congress in 1927, and a similar fate soon befell the Right Opposition of Bukharin, Rykov and Tomsky. By 1930 Stalin had consummated the circular flow of power, and through it had achieved firm if not untroubled personal dictatorship.

The specific methods of central control over provincial politics established before and during Stalin's rise to power survive to the present. They include the "recommendation" of candidates for local party office; the control of potential appointees for these offices through the nomenklatura system; the use of the power of party discipline to remove officials who no longer serve the center effectively; the nation-wide transfer of centrally chosen candidates for local "election," including the rotation of apparatus assignments between the provinces and the Secretariat staff in Moscow; and the dispatch of high-ranking "instructors" and sometimes even members of the Secretariat to supervise provincial meetings and make sure that the center's choices are duly installed. The only variable has been the frequency of recourse to these methods, high during Stalin's rise in the twenties and during the transition of the fifties, lower under Brezhnev, high again during the post-Brezhnev transition.

The structure of the Communist Party leadership is the direct outcome of Stalin's successful climb to power. It was Stalin who converted first the Central Committee and then the Politburo into bureaucratic status groups based on office-holding, as he elevated his appointees to elite rank and eliminated the political personalities whom he had forced into opposition. He thereby introduced the finely drawn sense of rank and precedence that has pervaded Soviet officialdom ever since.

In Stalin's reconstruction of the Central Committee we thus have a concrete example of a mechanism by which traditional Russian political culture reasserted itself as an unacknowledged and perhaps even unconscious guide to political behavior under Communism. In this instance the mechanism was reinforced by the actual personalities involved—non-intellectual revolutionary undergrounders in the nineteen-twenties, young workers and peasants in the nineteen-thirties—who were recruited by Stalin to staff the postrevolutionary bureaucracy. Once in high office, these tough parvenus only knew how to conduct themselves and to measure their associates and underlings as old Russian peasants supposed all bureaucracies must.

The ultimate weakness of dictatorship based on the circular flow of power is its dependence on the personal longevity of the dictator. As a system for sustaining the power of the established leader, the circular flow served well in Stalin's time, intensified by the threat or actuality of physical liquidation of his subordinates. But with the death of the leader there was no automatic way either to identify a new boss or for an aspirant to that role to inherit the power that depended on the circular flow. Stalin's unique power died with him, and it was available to be recreated only to the extent that a successor could repeat the process of bureaucratic appointment, organizational manipulation, and self-confirmation.

In 1953 Nikita Khrushchev found himself as First Secretary in a vantage point very much the same as Stalin's in 1924. It therefore fell to him to try to replicate the circular flow of power and amass for himself true personal power as Stalin had. Khrushchev quickly proved himself an apt pupil, as he asserted control of the Secretariat and proceeded to remove and replace party secretaries at vulnerable points in the apparatus.[22] By 1955 he had a strong enough political base to ease his rival Malenkov out of the chairmanship of the Council of Ministers. The following year, observing the custom of recognizing new bureaucratic office-holders, he could dictate the membership of the Twentieth Party Congress and the new Central Committee to his satisfaction. Of the 125 members of 1952, he replaced 40 (28 in the party apparatus), in addition to the five vacancies created by natural death or execution. However, he was not yet ready to attack the Party Presidium (as the Politburo was called from 1952 to 1964) head-on, although his de-Stalinization campaign has often been explained as a move to provoke his Stalinist rivals. The circle of power was finally closed in mid-1957 after the crisis of the Anti-Party Group, when Khrushchev caused his challengers to be removed from their party and government posts, took control of the Party Presidium, and soon afterwards assumed the leadership of the government as well as of the party.

How then could Khrushchev have been deposed a few short years later? Retrospective evidence, including the unusual pattern of Central Committee selection in 1961 and 1966, suggests that he was the victim of a neo-Stalinist opposition in the party apparatus. Instead of challenging him vainly at the top party level as in 1957, Khrushchev's enemies evidently managed instead to break into the circular flow of power, and were thereby able to undermine the leader bureaucratically.[23] Judging by the pattern of personnel changes in the party apparatus, Khrushchev began to lose his grip as early as the winter of 1959–1960, as people he had installed between 1953 and 1956 were in turn replaced. This trend accelerated in 1960–1961, and was reflected in the extraordinary turnover in the Central Committee at the Twenty-Second Congress. Half of Khrushchev's men elected in 1956 were now dropped, along with half the members held over from 1952, though this housecleaning reflected in part the Stalinist casualties of 1957 and 1958. In any event, 1961 saw the highest rate of renovation in the top leadership between Stalin's death and the present time, not excepting Gorbachev's congress in 1986. Between drops and deaths and the increase in the Central Committee to 175, there were seats for 108 new members. But renovation at this juncture must not be confused with rejuvenation. The new cohort of 1961, with a median birth year of 1910, was just as old as the group it replaced had been at the previous congress; the post-purge generation was only confirmed in power.

Basically the upheaval of 1961 was not a matter of generational change but of factional realignment. The probability that the new wave of leadership represented anti-Khrushchev neo-Stalinists, not Khrushchevian reformers, is supported by the fact that the next Central Committee, in 1966, evidenced the lowest rate of turnover at any point in the post-Stalin era. Of the 108 newcomers of 1961, 85 were returned in 1966 (four having died). Thus the neo-Stalinists who were presumably brought into the Central Committee in 1961 as a reflection of anti-Khrushchev appointments in the bureaucracy were confirmed in office after he fell, and not removed as would have been expected had they been Khrushchev's protegés. The neo-Stalinist thesis accounts for the otherwise inexplicable aberrations in Central Committee turnover, both the very high figure of 1961 and the very low one of 1966. In sum, the neo-Stalinists, led first by Kozlov and then by Brezhnev, with Suslov playing the grey eminence behind both, succeeded in redirecting the circular flow of power to undermine the party leader, get control of the Central Committee, and ultimately accomplish a palace revolution for the first and so far only time in the Soviet era.

The overthrow of Khrushchev did not reopen the question of the top leadership and the circular flow of power as the death of Stalin had done. In this case, the circular flow to confirm new authority had already been going on before the actual transition, in the course of the neo-Stalinists' machinations between 1959 and 1964. Furthermore, the instigator of the new power flow was not an individual but a cabal. After

Khrushchev's removal, the circular flow actually slowed down, as the people who had participated in it prior to 1964 consolidated their positions. These were among the conditions that governed the relatively greater continuity and collectivity of leadership in the Brezhnev era. It remained for the death of Brezhnev and the senescence of the post-purge generation in the 1980s to reopen the politics of the circular flow in a classic instance of the process.

4. The Brezhnev Era and Participatory Bureaucracy

It is ironic that the era dominated by the post-purge generation of Stalin's disciples proved to be the time of Soviet Russia's most consistent approximation of the principle of collective leadership. Though Brezhnev's rule was based on a conservative reaction against the excesses of Khrushchevian reformism, it originated in the altogether un-Stalinist overthrow of the top leader. This in turn implied the removability of that leader's successors and the ultimate supremacy of a bureaucratic group—scarcely Stalinist ideas.

Consistent with this fundamental change, Soviet politics since 1964 appear to have been governed by a sort of balance of power and consensus-seeking among several political levels, including the General Secretary, the upper oligarchy (i.e., the Politburo), and the broad bureaucratic leadership at the level of the Central Committee. This has not meant a dismantling of central authority or a retreat from the principle of party control, as an exaggerated interest-group interpretation might imply. What seems to have taken hold is a process of representation and balancing of functional bureaucratic interests, going on under the broad umbrella of party authority and decision-making. This is the system that I have termed "participatory bureaucracy."[24]

Continuity, everyone agrees, was the hallmark of the Brezhnev era. The post-purge generation of leadership, passing from its fifties to its sixties, was ensconced for a prolonged heyday, protected both by its own life expectancy and by the new political balance in the system. The circular flow of power slowed down, job-tenure membership in the elite was confirmed, and participatory bureaucracy brought the status-quo interests of the upper officialdom strongly into the policy-making process. Against all these circumstances there was only limited opportunity to make natural replacements among the leadership, given the median age of the Central Committee in 1966 of only 56. All the unwritten rules of Soviet politics—promotion tracks, representational entitlements, rights to status, and the balance of function and prestige—were repeatedly and deeply confirmed.

TABLE 7
Survival in the Central Committee, by Entry Cohort

Entry Year of Cohort	Central Committee							
	1952	1956	1961	1966	1971	1976	1981	1986
1952[a]	125	79	40	36	23	15	12	3
1956		54	27	23	18	13	7	4
1961			108	85	69	57	38	13
1966				51	40	35	29	10
1971					91	81	67	32
1976						86	77	50
1981							89	60
1986								135
Total	125	133	175	195	241	287	319	307

[a]For purposes of this analysis, the 125 members of 1952 are treated as one entry cohort,
although 34 of them actually entered in 1939 or earlier.

Given these conditions, there is little wonder that the Brezhnev era
was distinguished by the continuity in leadership documented so clearly
in the high rate of retention of Central Committee members following
the turmoil of the Khrushchev era. (See Table 1 and Table 7.) Yet
continuity did not mean, as is often suggested, that a fixed leadership
group held office until death knocked at the door. A steady though
modest rate of turnover went on in the Central Committee, after the
unusual continuity of 1966 that reflected the consolidation of the 1961
cohort of new members. Thanks in part to the steady expansion of the
body (accomplished largely by upgrading Candidate-rank jobs to full
membership), new members in 1971, 1976, and 1981 constituted 37%,
30%, and 28% of the respective Central Committees. As a result of
expansion and replacement, the Central Committee always had a majority
of members who were only in their first or second terms (even in 1981,
when the "upperclassmen" were one seat short of a majority). However,
well over half of the new members between 1966 and 1981 had served
one or more terms as Candidate members or members of the CAC, in
contrast to the direct installation of the great majority of the new
members in 1956, in 1961, and again in 1986.

Brezhnev's personnel choices did not entirely exclude younger people,
contrary to the general impression. The median age for new members
installed directly, without service at Candidate or CAC rank, stayed in
the range of 49 to 53 for each congress down to 1981, and only went
up to the high of 55 in 1986. But these new people were outweighed
by those promoted from the lower ranks, who were closer in age to the
holdovers in each Central Committee. Overall, only a decade in median

age separated the new entrants to full membership in 1961 and in 1981, twenty years apart. (See Table 2.) Drops were not numerous enough and new cohorts were not young enough on the average to prevent the median age of the Central Committee from creeping steadily upwards until 1981.

At the same time, a growing age spread was introduced between the aging old hands and the more youthful members of the new cohorts. The span in median age between the oldest and youngest quartiles of the membership widened from 57–49 in 1961 (eight years) to 70–55 in 1981 (fifteen years). 40% of the 1981 Central Committee had been under 30 when Stalin died. This was not exactly a guarantee of liberalism, among people who had by that age already gone through the Komsomol and party cadre screening process, but it was at least a measure of how far the generation of the most hard-bitten Stalinists had been diluted. It may also be significant that ever since 1961 the contingent of Central Committee members from the party apparatus has been kept consistently three to four years younger than the overall median,[25] while the governmental and military people have regularly averaged older than the norm. Even so, the median age for party apparatus members crept up at the same rate as the Central Committee as a whole, from 49.5 in 1961 to 59 in 1981.

We naturally know very little about real politics at the top level of the Soviet structure, except by inference. We are balked here by the unwritten law, rooted in old Russian political culture, calling for the suppression of any public evidence of individuality and disagreement among the leaders.[26] Nevertheless there appears to be a genuine political process of deals, threats, and coalitions going on in the upper reaches of the system, laterally as well as vertically, to arrive at decisions on both personnel and policy.

Where preponderant and final power is located in this Byzantine system is another question that defies precise answer. Comparing Stalin's times with Brezhnev's, power has clearly spread from individuals to committees and from the top downwards, though how far we cannot say. Certainly the Central Committee has a potent function, through the local and specialized bureaucracies that its members direct as well as through its role as ultimate arbiter in a struggle for power at the top. We may presume that the same sharing of the decision-making power works further down, as government ministers and provincial party secretaries accommodate their constituencies to avert dissension that might undermine their own positions in the eyes of the top leadership. Thus the mutual vulnerability of leader and oligarchy leads to an inclusion of lower levels of officialdom in the real power process, as those above maneuver for support below. This is not competitive electoral politics in the familiar Western sense, but it bears analogy with the bureaucratic politics that go on in every hierarchically organized entity in modern society.

5. The Generational Crisis and the Triple Succession

The death of Leonid Brezhnev in November 1982 signalled another unique era of change in Soviet political life. This transition was distinguished not merely by the demise of a leader and the necessity of recreating individual power, as in the succession to Stalin, but also by the passing of an entire dominant generation in the nation's top leadership bodies. Time finally caught up with the post-purge heirs of Stalinism, as death and debility opened the way for a generational revolution the like of which had not been seen since the time of the prewar purges. The crisis of biological limits was nowhere more evident than in the country's highest position, as the transfer of leadership first to one and then another representative of the old generation was foiled by death, leaving the field finally to a man two decades younger than his predecessors.

Generational politics undoubtedly figured in the surprise turns of the political wheel during the triple succession to Brezhnev. To challenge the favorite and Brezhnev's choice, Konstantin Chernenko, Yuri Andropov had to mobilize support in the Politburo and the Central Committee around the catalytic issues of discipline and reform.[27] By 1981, thanks to the modest but steady intake of younger members into the Central Committee, particularly in the contingent from the party apparatus, there was a substantial body of influential people who must have felt frustrated by the immobilism of policy under Brezhnev and repelled by the prospect of more of the same under Chernenko. Seweryn Bialer comments, "The new generation . . . are skeptical about the grander claims of Soviet propaganda concerning the system's merits. In private, they do not disguise their dislike of and lack of respect for the old generation."[28] This mood, together with the more obvious elements of military and police support, helps account for Andropov's dark horse victory following his surprising elevation to the Secretariat a few months before Brezhnev's death. If this theory is accurate, Andropov's success was a major victory for participatory bureaucracy, of power resting on the consent, if not of the governed, then at least of some of the key governors.

The unpredictable nature of Andropov's selection, like that of both Chernenko and Gorbachev following him, is indicative of the real politics that must have been going on behind the scenes in the Kremlin during the era of the triple succession. While there is, contrary to common opinion, a clear mechanism for determining the succession to the post of General Secretary—i.e., selection by the Politburo and ratification by the Central Committee—the process is indeterminate in the sense that the actual identity of the successor is not arrived at by any automatic formula. Rather, it is the outcome of political maneuver among powerful bureaucratic chieftains and their constituencies—again, participatory bureaucracy. To be sure, there is a constraint in yet another unwritten law, that the General Secretary must be chosen from among the three or four individuals who are simultaneously members of both the Politburo and the Party Secretariat. Nevertheless, the possibilities of maneuver allow ambitious members of the Politburo with "independent political resources" to secure seats in the Secretariat, as Andropov did in 1982 and Romanov in 1983, in order to position themselves for a bid for power.[29] The chance sequence of three closely-spaced vacancies in the office of General Secretary underscored the significance of genuinely fluid politics at the pinnacle of the system, and at the same time opened the process to more imput from below when aspirants for the leadership had to compete for bureaucratic support. Thus the ultimate locus of power would seem to be further diffused downward in a system that must be regarded as a complex oligarchy. This trend is not likely to be quickly reversed simply by the consolidation of a more stable leadership in the person of Gorbachev.

When Andropov succeeded Brezhnev, he immediately set the circular flow of power in motion once again, forcing resignations and making new appointments in jobs of Central Committee rank. He did not do this in an all-or-nothing fashion that could have provoked a threatening bureaucratic rebellion, but only proceeded step-by-step as obvious occasions arose. He did not disturb the Politburo at all except as death opened up the opportunity. Under the conservative Chernenko renovation slowed down to a crawl, but a start had been made.

On the basis of Andropov's initiatives, Gorbachev was able to resume and accelerate the circular flow of power when he assumed the General Secretaryship in March 1985. He launched a program of quick and sweeping changes in jobs of Central Committee rank both in the party and in the government. Between the Twenty-Sixth and Twenty-Seventh Congresses, of the replacements of Central Committee rank functionaries that can be dated, 27 were accomplished under Andropov, only 10 during Chernenko's thirteen months in office, and 57 in the year that elapsed between Gorbachev's installation as General Secretary and the convening of the Twenty-Seventh Congress. With this momentum Gorbachev was able to complete the circular flow by reaching into the Politburo itself and ousting those members—Romanov, Grishin, and Tikhonov—who had most conspicuously challenged or resisted him. The way was then open for him to carry through a renovation of the Central Committee at the forthcoming party congress such as had not been seen in a quarter-century.

6. The Twenty-Seventh Congress and the Implications of a New Generation

The Twenty-Seventh Party Congress was a signal event in several ways. It clearly confirmed the leadership of Gorbachev and his reform line as the outcome of the triple succession. In the Central Committee that it installed it consummated the generational overturn, with the passing of the post-purge leaders at all levels. At the same time, the congress confirmed the continuity of the forms and processes of political life that had marked the Soviet Union since the death of Stalin and in some respects since his rise.

A rich body of data in support of all these observations is the composition of the new Central Committee, elected unanimously, as is the custom, upon the nomination of a single slate on the last day of the congress. The prevailing job slot basis of membership selection, and the apportionment of seats according to the political importance of various bureaucratic functions and geographical areas, continued to be observed. The operation of the circular flow of power, simultaneously effecting the generational transition and undergirding the leadership position of Gorbachev and the reformers, was compellingly manifested in the number of new Andropov and Gorbachev appointees who won membership on the Committee—135 new people out of a total of 307 on the list of full members.

The 1986 Central Committee stands out in a number of ways against the trends of recent decades. For one thing, its numbers were reduced— from 319 to 307—for the first time ever in the history of the Soviet regime. Evidently the new leadership decided to call a halt to the progressive status inflation that had seen the Central Committee expand from 125 members in 1952 to its maximum of 319 in 1981, though the 1986 reduction was offset by an increase in the number of Candidate members from 151 to 170, the highest ever. Certain symbolic adjustments were made in the allocation of representation, notably a substantial increase in the number of mass representatives, the demotion of a number of central government ministries when their new incumbents were given only Candidate rank, and the rebuke to the Central Asian republics already noted. For the first time (except for marshals and former chiefs of state) a number of retired dignitaries were allowed to keep their seats, presumably so as to phase them out of office more gently than had been the custom. They included the ex-prime minister Tikhonov, the former First Deputy chief of state Kuznetsov, the ex-chairman of Gosplan Baibakov, and the retired party secretary and ideologist Ponomarev. Another secretary, Kapitonov, was moved to the Central Auditing Commission to serve as its new chairman with personal status more or less equivalent to Central Committee membership.

The increase in mass representatives, while the government representation was being cut, is evidently a sign that the leadership wants a more popular image. Moreover it hopes to overcome the impression that it excludes women, who were increased from 8 out of 319 (2.5%) in 1981 to 12 out of 307 (4%) in 1986. However, the increase occurred largely in the mass representative category and did not extend to significant inclusion of women in positions of actual power. Among the nationalities, the Gorbachev message is even more firmly one of Russian and Slavic hegemony, as shown by that preference in the mass representative category and by the carefully graduated downgrading of Central Asian representation in both the party and governmental sectors.

All these changes were merely expressions of fine tuning in the system. The great impact of the Twenty-Seventh Congress was in recognizing the extent of restaffing of the existing structure with people who were not only new but definitely younger. The 1986 Central Committee reflected the greatest percentage turnover of any since 1961, and was the first since 1952 to register an actual decrease in the median age of its members. The survivors of the post-purge generation were largely eliminated from the scene; of the 195 members of the first Brezhnev Central Committee, 86 of whom still held office in 1981, only 30 remained in 1986—barely a tenth of the new membership. This sifting left only 40 members born before 1918, which had been the median birth year for all members in 1981. Only three individuals remained from Stalin's last Central Committee of 1952 (Party Secretary Mikhail Zimianin, and retirees Baibakov and Kuznetsov), and only four from those who entered the Central Committee in 1956 (Gromyko, Ponomarev, Kazakhstan chief Dinmukhamed Kunaev, and the chairman of the People's Control Committee, A. M. Shkolnikov). (See Table 7.)

Turnover and renovation in Central Committee slots were even more striking when broken down according to functional categories. Youth and freshness were most evident in the party apparatus contingent, where power was concentrated. New appointments moved the median birth year in this group seven years later, from 1922 to 1929, for a net reduction in age of two years while five years were elapsing. The central government ministers, subject to extensive restaffing, showed a striking drop in median age, from 66 in 1981 to 61, but still remained on the average 4 years older than the party group. Other groups were either held to roughly the same age or were numerically insignificant (except for the cultural and educational leadership which actually went up in age).

In and of itself the Twenty-Seventh Congress did nothing decisive. But it did register the personal triumph of Gorbachev, for the time being, over any possible combination of older rivals. This was a victory that reflected and depended upon the advent of a new generation of bureaucrats who scored their success by waiting for the demographic revolution that had to come. In turn it opened the path to potential policy changes, presaged only by rhetoric at the congress, that might change the face of the country to a degree that can only be speculated about.

7. The Old System in New Hands

The history of Soviet politics since the death of Stalin is a story of change within a broader continuity. Despite the vicissitudes of individual leadership and the evolution of a more sophisticated—and more cynical—society, the structure of politics from 1953 to the present has remained essentially unchanged. Power has continued to reside in the uppermost levels of a highly centralized bureaucracy, though a certain balance has been reached among the various echelons. Firm rules of status and advancement have governed both the distribution of power and influence, and access to their enjoyment. In the long middle reach of this period, between 1961 and 1982, change both of personnel and of attitude proceeded as slowly as the longevity of individuals would allow. All of these conditions were reflected in the immobilism of the Brezhnev era.

On the other hand, there are certain systemic aspects of the Gorbachev succession, confirmed by the Twenty-Seventh Congress, that represent a break with the immediate past, at least in degree. While Gorbachev of necessity observed the job-slot system of leadership participation and the circular path to the consolidation of power, the opportunity afforded by the demographic exhaustion of the old leadership cadre gave the new General Secretary the chance to restaff all branches of the Soviet institutional structure at a more rapid rate than had ever been seen since World War II. This meant for him the possibility of amassing firmer personal influence than any Soviet leader since Stalin. Thereby he could achieve the political base necessary for any notable policy initiative.

For the immediate future Gorbachev has the opportunity as well as the need to press on with the circular flow of power through the appointment process. By the time of the next party congress in 1991 he may well succeed in replacing a majority of the 172 Brezhnev-era holdovers on the 1986 Central Committee, and perhaps accomplish a new reshuffling of the Politburo to establish a greater degree of personal dominance where he now shares power with a group of Andropov protegés. The issue of economic reform could well serve as the anvil on which these changes would be hammered out. Reform would in turn be advanced by the personnel changes made in its name. For structural reasons that may not yet be widely appreciated, Gorbachev could indeed become a major figure in this epoch of the history of Russia.

But uncertainties remain. There is the haunting lesson of the overthrow of Khrushchev. The traditions of job-slot representation and participatory bureaucracy limit how far and how fast the General Secretary can move, but they must be respected on pain of provoking a bureaucratic rebellion that could endanger the leader's tenure altogether. Gorbachev's position is delicate. He must continue to move the circular flow to make his personal dominance more meaningful than Brezhnev did, yet must not drive these changes so vigorously as to stir up the sort of concerted counter-offensive of participatory bureaucracy that was Khrushchev's undoing. Soviet politics at the top will continue for the foreseeable future to depend on the interplay of real politics among flesh-and-blood competitors for the sweet fruit of power.

Notes

1. T. H. Rigby, "The Structure of the Supreme Leadership, 1917–1985," in Archie Brown, ed., *Political Leadership in the Soviet Union* (London: Macmillan, 1988).

2. See John Miller, "Transitions to the Top: Cooptation into the Supreme Leadership since the Death of Stalin," ibid.

3. See Stephen White, *Political Culture and Soviet Politics* (New York: St. Martin's, 1979), esp. ch. 2 and 3, and "The USSR: Patterns of Autocracy and Industrialism," in Archie Brown and Jack Gray, eds., *Political Culture and Political Change in Communist States* (New York: Holmes and Meier, 1977).

4. The generational phenomenon is well described in Seweryn Bialer, *Stalin's Successors: Leadership, Stability, and Change in the Soviet Union* (Cambridge, England: Cambridge University Press, 1980), pp. 59–61, 86–89. Jerry Hough, in *Soviet Leadership in Transition* (Washington: Brookings, 1980), pp. 37–60, distinguishes four "generations" or more accurately sub-generations in the post-war Soviet leadership, based on their differing experiences of the purges and the war—the "Brezhnev generation" born in 1900–1909 who benefitted most from the purges; the slower-moving but better-educated cohort of 1910–1918; the war-time group born in 1919–1925 whose educations again fell short; and the post-war generation, born after 1925, a true elite educationally, and moreover less scarred by Stalinism. The "post-purge" generation described here is primarily Hough's first group and secondarily the second.

5. See T. H. Rigby, "Was Stalin a Disloyal Patron?" *Soviet Studies,* XXXVII:3 (July 1986).

6. This assumes that the nine one-time members whose birth year is unknown were distributed equally above and below the median. If they were preponderantly

younger the median would have been 48. Practically all ages of full members in subsequent cohorts are known. The time of year is ignored in computing median ages. Median ages are used in this analysis in preference to mean ages, as a more meaningful reflection of the balance of older and younger individuals.

7. Miller, "Transitions to the Top."

8. Sheila Fitzpatrick, "Stalin and the Making of the New Elite, 1928–1939," *Slavic Review*, XXXVIII:3 (September, 1979), pp. 377–402.

9. Edward L. Keenan, "Muscovite Political Folkways," *The Russian Review*, XV:2 (April 1986), pp. 167–169.

10. The mass representatives tend to be younger and to be replaced faster than the rest of the elite, and to that extent they skew the statistics. Some of them turn out to be rising trade union officials or industrial bureaucrats.

11. See Robert V. Daniels, "Office Holding and Elite Status: The Central Committee of the CPSU," in Paul Cocks, Robert V. Daniels, and Nancy Whittier Heer, eds., *The Dynamics of Soviet Politics* (Cambridge, Mass.: Harvard University Press, 1976).

12. Information from an East European journalist.

13. For a more extensive statement of this proposition, see John H. Kress, "Representation of Positions on the CPSU Politburo," *Slavic Review*, XXXIX:2 (June 1980), pp. 218–238.

14. I first spelled out the notion of the "circular flow of power" in "Stalin's Rise to Dictatorship," in Alexander Dallin and Alan F. Westin, eds., *Politics in the Soviet Union: Seven Cases* (New York: Harcourt, Brace and World, 1966), pp. 4–5. See also Robert V. Daniels, "Soviet Politics since Khrushchev," in John W. Strong, ed., *The Soviet Union under Brezhnev and Kosygin* (New York: Van Nostrand, 1971), pp. 20–21.

15. Lenin, "Svoboda kritiki i edinstvo deistviya" (Freedom of Criticism and Unity of Action, June 1906), *Sochineniia* (Works), 2nd ed. (Moscow: Marx-Engels-Lenin Institute, 1928), vol. IX, pp. 274–275. Lenin was defending himself against charges of indiscipline by those Social Democrats who were trying to reunite the Bolshevik and Menshevik factions. See Alfred G. Meyer, *Leninism* (Cambridge, Mass.: Harvard University Press, 1957), pp. 92–103.

16. See Ronald Tiersky, *Ordinary Stalinism: Democratic Centralism and the Question of Communist Political Development* (Boston: Allen and Unwin, 1985), esp. pp. 8, 42. One hint of reviving the democratic component was offered by the Soviet scholar A. P. Butenko in "Protivorechiya razviitiya sotsializma kak obshchestvennogo stroya" (Contradictions in the Development of Socialism as a Social Order), *Voprosy filosofii*, no. 16, 1982.

17. See Rigby, "The Structure of the Supreme Leadership."

18. See Robert V. Daniels, "The Secretariat and the Local Organizations in the Russian Communist Party," *The American Slavic and East European Review*, XVI:1 (February 1957).

19. Ibid., pp. 41–42.

20. See Robert V. Daniels, "Evolution of Leadership Selection in the Central Committee, 1917–1927," in Walter M. Pintner and Don K. Rowney, eds., *Russian Officialdom: The Bureaucratization of Russian Society from the Seventeenth to the Twentieth Century* (Chapel Hill: University of North Carolina Press, 1980).

21. Rigby, "The Structure of the Supreme Leadership."

22. I have detailed this process in an unpublished paper, "Khrushchev and the Party Secretaries," delivered at the Mid-West Slavic Conference, Columbus, Ohio, 1966.

23. For a more extensive discussion of this thesis see Daniels, "Soviet Politics since Khrushchev," pp. 21–22. See also Michel Tatu, *Power in the Kremlin from Khrushchev to Kosygin* (New York: Viking, 1969), pp. 33–37 et seq.; William Hyland and Richard W. Shryock, *The Fall of Khrushchev* (New York: Funk and Wagnalls, 1968), pp. 10–18.

24. Robert V. Daniels, "Participatory Bureaucracy and the Soviet Political System," in Norton T. Dodge, ed., *Analysis of the USSR's 24th Party Congress and 9th Five-Year Plan* (Mechanicsville, Md.: Cremona Foundation, 1971).

25. Bialer, *Stalin's Successors* (pp. 122–123), notes the surprising frequency of youthful (fortyish) first secretaries of provinces.

26. See Keenan, "Folkways," p. 170.

27. See Archie Brown, "Andropov: Discipline and Reform?" *Problems of Communism,* XXXII:1 (January–February 1983).

28. Seweryn Bialer, "The Political System," in Robert F. Byrnes, ed., *After Brezhnev: Sources of Soviet Conduct in the 1980s* (Bloomington: Indiana University Press, 1983), p. 23.

29. Miller, "Transitions to the Top."

6

The Intelligentsia
and the Success of Reform:
From Brezhnev to Gorbachev

Two decades after the debacle of reform under the aegis of Nikita Khrushchev, the Soviet Union has reached another opening in its political life. This time the opportunity for change has been presented not merely by the demise of a leader wedded to cultural orthodoxy and control, but by the passing of an entire generation of leadership brought up in the school of Stalinist postrevolutionary self-justification. With Brezhnev, Andropov, Chernenko, and their age-mates, the party and state officialdom who as a group had been growing old in high office since World War II began rapidly to die off or invite removal for age and disability. Gorbachev won the General Secretaryship in March 1985, not merely as a youthful symbol of renovation, but as the physical representative of a new generation in charge of the Soviet Ship of State. Now the country's oldest political habits—"a philosophy of forbidding and re-stricting, a passion for banning things"[1]—are under attack, not by a revolutionary movement, but by the leadership of the state power itself.

The policy changes and leadership shifts effected by Gorbachev since his advent to power in 1985 already represent one of the most profound transitions experienced by the Soviet Union since the revolution. A happy combination of need, opportunity, and pressure made this turnabout possible. The need lay in the country's undeniable loss of momentum in economic growth and international prestige. The opportunity was the generational revolution in the Soviet political elite. Finally, the pressure was supplied by the force of the maturing intelligentsia and the intolerable discrepancy between the regime's revolutionary pretensions and its postrevolutionary reality.

The heart of Gorbachev's response to these circumstances was to reverse the traditional relationship between the holders of power and the intelligentsia. How deep or enduring this change may be, we cannot say at the present time. But Gorbachev's promises of reform are supported by certain basic historical forces, including the spread of an alternative political culture and the unfulfilled legacy of the revolution itself. He appears to have recognized that the liberation of the intelligentsia from the constraints of state power is the key to reform and national progress, and that only a free intelligentsia can make his "restructuring" "irreversible."

1. Neo-Stalinism and the Scientific-Technical Revolution

The years of Leonid Brezhnev's leadership, now so universally denigrated, were actually a time of contradictory developments in the relationship between the Soviet bureaucracy and the intelligentsia. To be sure, neo-Stalinism prevailed politically, as the post-purge cohort of leaders perpetuated the basic mentality of Stalinism in Soviet politics for more than a quarter of a century after Stalin himself had left the scene. On the other hand, faced like the tsarist bureaucracy in the nineteenth century with the challenge of continuing the modernization of the country and competing in the arena of international power, the neo-Stalinist bureaucracy could not escape sowing the seeds of its own destruction.

The crack in the monolith most apparent to the outside world was the confrontation between the bureaucracy and the creative intelligentsia that marked the Brezhnev era and worsened towards its end. Typically, representatives of the bureaucratic interest and outlook were installed or maintained in the nominal institutions of intellectual leadership, especially the unions of writers and other artistic categories. Repression of creative individuality, ranging from simple censorship or refusal to publish, all the way to arrest, trial, and imprisonment or exile, put an end to the relative freedom of the thaw of the 1950s and early 1960s, and effectively drove the new surge of creative effort underground. In the best Stalinist style, Brezhnev told the Twenty-Third Party Congress in March 1966, "We are unfailingly guided by the principal of party spirit in art and a class approach to the evaluation of everything that is done in the sphere of culture."[2] For Voznesensky the Brezhnev regime meant the "collapse of illusions."[3] The turning point was the arrest of Sinyavsky and Daniel in September 1965, and their trial and imprisonment in January 1966.[4]

The renewal of political repression did not suffice to maintain the constraints of the official doctrine of Socialist Realism on artistic form. "In the past two decades," wrote the literary historian Deming Brown in 1978, "there have been so many inroads into this doctrine in actual

practice as to render it virtually inoperative. . . . Socialist Realism
. . . has largely been replaced by critical realism."[5] For N. N. Shneidman
this meant the direct treatment of real human issues, "problems without
solutions," and the non-ideological question of "the ethical foundation
of Soviet Man."[6] Writers who stayed within the official limits were often
able to exert significant unofficial influence on government policy, as in
the movement to preserve historic buildings and the ultimately successful
protest against the diversion of Siberian rivers to Central Asia. As Soviet
intellectual life grew more mature and complex, it became more and
more difficult to practice the Stalinist habits of minute control and
direction from the top down.

The 1960s and 1970s were a time of vast numerical expansion in the
Soviet intelligentsia, particularly in the scientific and technical areas.
The Soviet leadership finally came to appreciate the complex evolution
of modern (or "post-modern") industrialism known in the USSR as the
"scientific-technical revolution." In consequence it had to respond to
the growing significance of the intelligentsia as a source of national
power and progress. According to Suslov, speaking as the chief ideologist
of the Brezhnev regime, "The contemporary scientific-technical revolution
opens before society unseen possibilities in using science for mastering
and protecting the forces of nature and solving social problems . . . ,
and at the same time acts as material preparation for communist
civilization."[7] Thus the "scientific-technical revolution" became an article
of official faith, even though its full implications were never thoroughly
defined. Cyril Black has termed it "the most important development in
Soviet ideology since 1917."[8]

Confidence in science and technological innovation as forces for
progress and betterment of the human condition has been axiomatic for
the Soviet regime from the beginning. This is one basic belief which
the Stalinist political class has preserved from the tradition of the
nineteenth-century intelligentsia, via the quasi-intelligentsia of the revolutionary era. Science is an area where the interests and outlook of
the Soviet bureaucracy and the intelligentsia are substantially congruent,
more clearly so after Stalin's personal interventions in scientific theory
became a thing of the past.

The conditions of scientific work in the Soviet Union improved
markedly in the 1950s and 1960s. Politically, the blantant imposition of
party doctrine on scientific conclusions came to an end, even though
Khrushchev continued to patronize the quack biological doctrines of
Trofim Lysenko until his downfall. With the growing importance and
complexity of science, the political leadership recognized implicitly that
it could not dictate scientific methods or conclusions. "Step by step the
Stalinist unity of science and ideology was dismantled," Alexander

Vucinich concludes, even though no "structural break" took place.[9] As a result, scientists and other specialists won a significant and growing degree of autonomy and influence, including the possibility of relatively free professional discussions.[10] Jerry Hough has noted "the gradual broadening of open policy debates by those who are willing to work within the system."[11] In this respect, the maturation of Soviet science foreshadowed the autonomy that was to come for other fields of intellectual endeavor under Gorbachev.

In the material respect, the post-Stalin decade saw, in the words of Eugene Zaleski, "an enormous expansion of the Soviet research and development effort,"[12] as well as of the educational base to support it. Soviet statistics, whatever their accuracy, give a rough measure of the rate of growth: 37,000 engineers graduated in 1950, 170,000 in 1965;[13] the number of all specialists graduating with higher education, 177,000 in 1950, 343,000 in 1960, 631,000 in 1970 (for a total employed by then of almost 7,000,000).[14] According to Vucinich, the total number of scientists doubled between 1947 and 1960, and doubled again between 1960 and 1966, though at the cost of a considerable dilution of quality.[15] "A wholesale approach was taken in developing the higher school," wrote the present editor of *Pravda*, V. G. Afanasiev. "Many universities that were hastily established for official reasons of prestige . . . have found themselves in a particularly difficult situation."[16]

By the 1970s there was actually an over-supply of experts in relation to what the Soviet economy could absorb. Zhores Medvedev has referred to "hypertrophy" and "redundancy" in the scientific establishment, particularly as exemplified in the creation of union-republic branches of the Academy of Sciences.[17] Afanasiev protested "talk of a surplus of highly trained specialists," but conceded, "The desire far exceeds the need," thanks to "the higher prestige that attaches to the intellectual professions." In consequence, "A certain disproportion has appeared in the system of education and professional training of the working people of the USSR. While we have an overabundance (from the standpoint of present needs) of highly trained specialists, there is a shortage of workers, and particuarly skilled workers."[18] This was the circumstance giving rise to the abortive Khrushchev education reform of 1958 and again to the education reform adopted under Chernenko in 1984, both measures endeavoring to restrict access to the intelligentsia and steer Soviet youth toward production at the bench. The same situation of competitiveness may also have contributed to the pattern of discrimination in admitting persons of Jewish nationality or even partial Jewish ancestry to intellectual jobs, and made this sacrifice of quality more tolerable. Nevertheless, Jews, maintaining a century-long tradition of intellectual ambition, have continued to be needed and represented in the research establishment well beyond their proportion in the population as a whole,[19] though the bureaucracy, according to one *samizdat* writer, dislikes "smartness" and considers Jews "too smart altogether."[20]

Despite its growth and the vital character of its services, the intelligentsia as a whole did not achieve in the 1960s and 1970s either the material or political conditions of life that would satisfy it. While a few outstanding scientists and politically conforming writers and personalities in the performing arts were rewarded with spectacularly high incomes and accompanying privilege, the rank and file of professional personnel—engineers, physicians, teachers, etc.—earned scarcely more than industrial workers (and less than miners and drivers), despite their extensive training. Thanks to salary compression in the 1960s as manual workers' pay caught up, the remuneration of scientific researchers was only 50% above the average for industrial workers; for engineers, it was only 10% above.[21] Tatyana Zaslavskaya, now a leading theoretician of "restructuring," recently commented, "The salaries of scientific and other creative personnel have not changed since the 1950s. . . . This is a reflection of the short-sighted policy of wage control, which ignores the fact that it is primarily the labor of scientists and engineers that forms the basis of scientific and technical progress. The inadequate material incentives for their work have led to a decline in its social prestige, diminished competition for admission to higher technical schools, a lower level for training of engineers in the country, and then to the slowing of scientific and technical progress and the growth of labor productivity."[22] As time went on, the lure of intelligentsia status failed more and more to compensate for inadequate income, and the conditions of life—cramped housing, waiting in line, scrounging for necessities—that most of the intelligentsia shared with more humble citizens manifestly contributed to the demoralization that grew steadily during the Brezhnev years. These conditions created a recruitment problem for the intelligentsia as a whole, and by the 1970s disaffected intellectuals often chose to take manual jobs, the slight economic loss being more than offset by the gain in personal independence.

Notwithstanding its tremendous expansion and growing sophistication, the Soviet effort in science, technology, and education still suffers from some long-standing limitations, reflecting the penetration of the bureaucratic culture into intellectual life. Soviet intellectual work is hierarchical and centralized, with a sharp pyramid of quality, prestige, and rewards. Geographically the overwhelming focus is Moscow, and secondarily Leningrad; assignment to work outside the centers is commonly felt by Soviet intellectuals as administrative exile. (The regime has acceded to this sentiment by allowing a disproportionate share of higher education and research, perhaps 10% of the total national effort, to concentrate in Moscow.[23]) The official mania for secrecy has balked the exchange of ideas, not only with the outside world but among Soviet scientists themselves (a danger to which security-conscious Western countries are not immune). Contact among institutes and disciplines, between researchers and teachers, and between pure research activity and the applied needs of industry is artificially restricted by organizational rigidity and traditions of specialization. The organization of Soviet scientific and intellectual life suggests a honeycomb, where communication between one cell and another, going upwards to some point of authority and then downwards through bureaucratic channels, is inordinately difficult. Soviet scholars in the same field, in the same city, but in different institutions, often simply do not know each other.

Theory and the theoretical disciplines, above all mathematics and physics, have traditionally been Russia's strong side intellectually. They still enjoy a great advantage in prestige over work of practical application. This circumstance and the relative immunity of such fields from political interference help account for the attraction of the most creative and critical minds to the theoretical sciences, which consequently became the seedbed for some of the boldest expressions of dissidence in the 1960s and after. In addition, as the emigré physicist Valentin Turchin has pointed out, there is the special attraction of science—and one might add, for Russia, the realm of artistic creativity—to "a certain type of personality requiring the existence of a higher goal . . . in other words, a religious type of person."[24]

Will the scientific-technical revolution have a significant impact on political life in the USSR? Officially it has been maintained that the STR will do nothing but enhance the building of communism. Many Western observers, on the other hand, argue that the requirements of technical innovation and information flow will compel the Soviet bureaucracy to loosen its centralist controls, and, as Eric Hoffmann predicts, "to broaden and deepen specialist elite participation at all stages and levels of decision making."[25] The direction of Gorbachev's economic reforms certainly appears to bear out this prediction. It is the familiar effect of changes in the mode of production—in this instance the high technology of the "post-industrial" era—generating pressures for change in the superstructure of economic and political organization. This puts more and more influence into the hands of the intelligentsia as the growingly dominant class, in influence and indispensability to the state as well as in numbers. Observes Hoffmann, "Technocratic consciousness becomes pervasive and subtly influences policy makers and information specialists thinking about politics."[26] To be sure, history amply demonstrates how an overgrown state power can frustrate the operation of rising social forces, but only at a great price in national energy, morale, and creativity. Russia has been compelled to pay that price too often in the past; the signs of the moment suggest that it will decline to do so in the future.

2. Dissidents, *Samizdat,* and the Democratic Movement

The political tension and cultural incompatibility between the bureaucracy and the intelligentsia or at least its creative stratum became dramatically evident in the various currents of dissent that took form after the fall of Khrushchev and the end of the post-Stalin thaw. Since that time the Soviet intellectual scene has been constantly punctuated by attempts at unregulated expression and corresponding acts of repression by the political authorities, stopping short of Stalin-type mass terror to be sure, but nevertheless sufficing until the advent of Gorbachev to prevent the intelligentsia from expressing itself in an independent, organized movement.

There is an obvious parallel between Soviet dissent and the Russian intelligentsia in the nineteenth century. Then as now dissent arose from the class that was relatively privileged and necessary to the state, but at the same time driven to independent-mindedness by virtue of its training and tradition, in other words its culture. Andrei Amalrik calculated that of the more than 700 individuals who signed petitions of protest in 1968, only 6% were workers, the others all being intellectuals or professionals.[27] Active dissidents tended to be youthful, and were disproportionately drawn from the literary and scientific milieux. Children of Stalin's purge victims, both political and cultural, were prominent among them. The only forms of articulate dissent that found a wider popular base were those of a religious or national-minority character (notably in the Baltic republics and among the Crimean Tatars). In the broadest sense, dissidence was a product of the unresolved contradictions between a changing society and a rigid political system, between the intelligentsia as the increasingly dominant class and the bureaucracy as a ruling class on the defensive.

Thanks to the constraints of censorship, as in the nineteenth century, the principal vehicle for dissent in the Brezhnev era was literature. Writers, enjoying unusual prestige compared with Western and particularly North American societies, again assumed their role as the nation's conscience, insofar as they could bring their thoughts to the attention of the reading public. Literary works that could not be tailored to the party's requirements for official publication were disseminated privately in the celebrated form of *samizdat*—"self-publishing"—usually accomplished by typing multiple carbon copies which in turn could be copied and multiplied by friends, a little like the transmission of learning by monastic copyists in the Middle Ages. It proved to be not very difficult to smuggle manuscripts abroad and allow them to be published, both in Russian and in foreign translation. This came to know as *tamizdat*—"publishing over there." Samizdat and tamizdat materials were broadcast back by Western radio services and reached much wider audiences, despite Soviet efforts to jam the transmissions. The radio in turn gave rise to *magnitizdat*—recording broadcasts with tape recorders (in Russian, *magnitofon*) and circulating them on tapes. Not surprisingly, magnitizdat spread from literary and political materials to officially disapproved forms of Western popular music, and the unofficial works of Soviet balladeers and other disfavored musicians as well. Bolder expressions of dissent included literary meetings, poetry readings, and actual political demonstrations. The latter invariably brought on police repression.

The opening gun in the bureaucracy's post-Khrushchev campaign to curb the intelligentsia was the Sinyavsky–Daniel affair. The case prompted a series of protests by intellectuals who saw it as a step toward the possible rehabilitation of Stalin, and led to a continuous dialectic of protests, repressions, and more protests over the next four years. On Soviet Constitution Day, December 5, 1965, the first of many short-lived demonstrations took place in Pushkin Square in Moscow when two hundred students from Sinyavsky's institute, the Gorky Institute of World Literature, gathered to protest the arrests and to demand a public trial. The trial and conviction of Sinyavsky and Daniel in January and February, 1966, prompted an unprecedented series of petitions signed by leading literary figures and scientists (including Andrei Sakharov in his first manifestation of political dissent), addressed to the Twenty-Third Party Congress. They may have helped avert the literal rehabilitation of Stalin, but the authorities did not hesitate to toughen the law against dissent by adding the infamous articles 190–191 and 190–193 to the criminal code, outlawing the dissemination of "political slander" and the holding of unauthorized demonstrations, respectively. This did not deter Alexander Ginzburg, a victim of repression in the late 1950s for attempting to publish the first samizdat journal, from compiling and circulating an unofficial transcript of the Sinyavsky–Daniel trial. For this he was arrested in January 1967, along with the writer Yuri Galanskov, who had run afoul of the KGB for preparing the samizdat literary anthology *Phoenix-66*. This step prompted another demonstration in Pushkin Square, organized by a group including the poet Vladimir Bukovsky (already the victim of two years' incarceration in a mental hospital) and the mathematician Alexander Yesenin-Volpin (son of the noted poet of the 1920s Sergei Yesenin). The inevitable outcome was more arrests and trials, and a deepening sense of agitation among wide circles of the intelligentsia.

At this point, Alexander Solzhenitsyn, whose own novels *The Cancer Ward* and *The First Circle* had been denied publication and forced into samizdat distribution, took the lead to protest the tightening curbs on the intelligentsia. Denied a chance to speak at the Fourth Writers' Congress in May 1967, Solzhenitsyn launched into a running battle of letters with the leadership of the Writers' Union, to no avail. Bukovsky and the demonstrators of January 1967 were put on trial in August, and Bukovsky got three years for his uncompromising defiance. Then in January 1968, the subjects of that protest, Ginzburg and Galanskov, were tried and convicted on the familiar charge of anti-Soviet slander.

These moves provoked even broader protests, distinguished by the participation of Pavel Litvinov, the physicist grandson of the Foreign Commissar, and Pyotr Yakir, son of the purged Red Army general Iona Yakir, together with the dissident Major General Pyotr Grigorenko. Yakir and his friends warned in an open letter to the international Communist conference then being held in Budapest, "For several years ominous symptoms of a restoration of Stalinism have been evident in the life of our society. . . . We have no guarantees that the year 1937 will not come upon us again."[28] The *Chronicle of Current Events*, recording dissident activities and repressions, began to appear in samizdat in April 1968. At the same time Sakharov took the lead in the dissident movement by distributing his essay, "Progress, Coexistence, and Intellectual Freedom," in which he reviewed the evils of Stalinism and called for fundamental political reform. None of these challenges deterred the authorities, spurred on by a Central Committee resolution of April 1968 on fighting "anti-Communist propaganda," from stepping up their campaign of warnings, searches, and arrests of dissident intellectuals.

The confrontation between regime and dissidents was intensified by the Soviet intervention in Czechoslovakia in August 1968, which snuffed out a political evolution among the more Western-style Communists of Prague and Bratislava remarkably similar to the program of reform that Soviet intellectuals were pressing for. Grigorenko and his friends immediately circulated a statement of protest, and on August 25, four days after the invasion, a group led by Pavel Litvinov and Yuli Daniel's wife Larissa Bogoraz demonstrated in Red Square, only to be immediately beaten and arrested by the KGB. They were put on trial with dispatch, in October, and sentenced to terms of Siberian exile. Similar protests in Leningrad and other provincial centers were disposed of with corresponding harshness.

During the next two years the bureaucratic noose steadily tightened around the dissident intelligentsia. Among the notable acts of police repression in this period were the arrest of Grigorenko (for supporting the Crimean Tatars), the expulsion of Solzhenitsyn from the Writers' Union (for the publication of *The Cancer Ward* in Italy), the removal of Tvardovsky from the editorship of *Novyi Mir*, the arrest of Andrei Amalrik (for publishing *Will the Soviet Union Survive until 1984?*), and the brief commitment of the biologist Zhores Medvedev to a mental hospital (for publishing his expose of Lysenkoism[29]). Nevertheless the dissident movement continued to attract supporters and to assume a steadily more organized and programmatic form. In May 1969, the Initiative Group for the Defense of Human Rights in the USSR, led by Yakir, attempted to appeal to the United Nations about the treatment of Soviet dissidents. Sakharov, Turchin, and Roy Medvedev issued a "Manifesto" to the Soviet leadership in March 1970 calling for the democratization of the system, and in October of the same year Sakharov and Chalidze created the Committee for Human Rights in the USSR, described by Ludmilla Alexeyeva as "the first independent association [of dissidents] with parliamentary procedures and rules of membership."[30] The Democratic Movement was at the point of becoming a coherent vehicle of the aspirations of the Soviet intelligentsia.

Caught between this challenge and the potential international embarrassment in the era of détente if they continued their earlier tactics of repression, the Soviet authorities began in 1972 to employ a very new approach to the dissident intellectuals. This was to decapitate the movement by allowing its most prominent members to emigrate abroad, or even to deport them forcibly and deprive them of Soviet citizenship. Apart from non-returners who went abroad on ostensibly temporary missions and lost their citizenship, the first case where this tactic was employed was that of one of the earliest victims of neo-Stalinist repression, the poet Joseph Brodsky, released from prison and deported in 1972. During the next two years a series of eminent dissidents was allowed or pressured to leave, including Chalidze, Sinyavsky, Litvinov, the balladeer Alexander Galich, and cellist Mstislav Rostropovich. Zhores Medvedev was deprived of his citizenship while on a research visit to England in 1973. The most sensational application of the method of expulsion was the case of Solzhenitsyn, whose defiance—deliberate publication abroad of his novel *August 1914* in 1971, and dissemination of his "Letter to the Soviet Leaders" in the fall of 1973—had become utterly intolerable to the authorities. In March 1974 he was seized and placed on a plane for West Germany, to begin an even more famous career in exile.

Despite the attempt by the authorities to eliminate the leadership of the Democratic Movement, it readily found new recruits, particularly as a result of the Helsinki Accords of August 1975, and the promises by all signatories including the USSR to respect basic democratic and human rights. In the spring of 1976 Sakharov and yet another physicist, Yuri Orlov, a Corresponding Member of the Academy, founded the Moscow Helsinki Watch Group to try to hold the Soviet authorities to this commitment. This in turn inspired a series of similar efforts in the union republics and among religious groups. Solzhenitsyn, using the royalties from his publications in the West, created the Russian Fund to aid Political Prisoners, administered in Moscow by Alexander Ginzburg, and in January 1977, the Working Commission to Investigate the Use of Psychiatry for Political Purposes was announced. These steps represented the high point of organized, open dissidence in the Brezhnev era.

During the early months of 1977, on the pretext of an explosion in the Moscow Metro attributed to "terrorists," the regime began an intense crackdown on the Helsinki Watch movement. Orlov, Ginzburg, and Anatoli Shcharansky (already a leading advocate of Jewish emigration rights) were among those arrested. Defying the Belgrade conference of late 1977 on the observance of the Helsinki Accords—"the first international meeting on a governmental level in which the Soviet Union was accused of human rights violations," in the words of Ludmilla Alexeyeva—the authorities followed through with trials and further arrests. Alexeyeva comments, "The dilemma facing the Soviet government had become quite obvious: either it lost prestige in the West or lost control over its own citizens. The government preferred to sacrifice its prestige."[31]

By 1980 the human rights movement had been effectively suppressed, certainly as an organized phenomenon. Nevertheless the regime had moderated its methods compared with the Stalin era and even with the late 1960s, preferring foreign exile or mental hospital commitment to the traditional sanctions of trial and imprisonment. Some dissidents, including Bukovsky in 1976 and Ginzburg in 1980 (as well as Shcharansky in 1985) were actually traded for captured Soviet agents or imprisoned Western Communists. Other intellectual figures forced to emigrate during the final Brezhnev years included Amalrik, the novelist Vasili Aksyonov, the satirist Vladimir Voinovich, and the sculptor Ernst Neizvestny. Finally, the sanction of internal exile to a closed city was imposed on Sakharov, when he was forcibly resettled early in 1980 in the industrial center of Gorki, under constant surveillance by the KGB, to choke off his contacts with the Western press and deprive the dissident movement of his leadership.

In the early Brezhnev years the common goals of intellectual freedom and survival against repression gave the dissident intelligentsia a strong sense of unity and cohesion. Later, and particularly in the freer circumstances of foreign exile, sharp political differences appeared among them.

Roughly three main tendencies emerged, led respectively by Solzhenitsyn, Sakharov, and Roy Medvedev. On the Right, Solzhenitsyn represented the appeal to traditional Russian culture and religion, with authoritarian and anti-Western overtones that quickly alienated most people in his country of refuge, the United States. The center was represented by Sakharov, whose defense of democratization and human rights put him in the camp of Western liberalism, very much like the Westernizers of the mid-nineteenth century. Dissidence of the Left was represented by Roy Medvedev, accepting the socialist premises of the revolution and aspiring to work within the system to reform it—"socialism with a human face," in essence. Not unlike prerevolutionary days, the polemics and struggles in the emigration between the adherents of these diverse views soon reached a point of bitterness that destroyed any semblance of a united front against the existing Soviet regime.

Under the circumstances of censorship and police repression against which it struggled, the movement of intellectual dissent was never able to bring its message to the mass of the population effectively enough to win their sympathy (apart from the religious and nationality exceptions noted earlier). Typically the non-intellectual Russian population rejected the dissidents as unpatriotic complainers, or even dismissed them all as Jews in disguise. Russia was experiencing an irreconcilable clash of cultures, as long as the bureaucracy continued to impose its values and to cultivate the innate authoritarianism and xenophobia of the less educated masses. Meanwhile the county was paying an inestimable price in the loss of creative talent, either through the braindrain of emigration or defection, or the silencing and demoralization of the best thinking people who remained at home. Sooner or later it would prove impossible for the bureaucracy to sustain its archaic political culture and maintain Russia's international standing by any criterion other than armed might.

3. The Intelligentsia, the Succession, and Perestroika

By the end of the Brezhnev era a variety of forces were working against the continued power of the neo-Stalinist bureaucracy. The cultivation of moderization, the expansion of the intelligentsia, and the need to rely on its expertise all made constant and detailed political interference counterproductive if not impossible. The conservatism of the post-purge leadership was losing all credibility, and the generation that sustained it was dying off. The old guard became mired in disbelief, corruption, and the stagnation that flowed from the fear of change. The intelligentsia, for its part, saw its hopes and spirit fading, and joined in the common pursuit of material success or mere survival. The historian

STAGNATION

Volodin recently acknowledged "the negative, and often corrupting effects of the 'deformative' factors of a more recent [post-Stalin] time in which bureaucratic and essentially unsocialist actions drained away active participation in sociopolitical life on the part of certain groups of the intelligentsia."[32] Nevertheless, the potential for change remained in the enduring traditions of the intelligentsia, now being absorbed in part by the new, more sophisticated cadre of leaders rising through the bureaucracy.

Could the bureaucratic culture not have perpetuated itself by continued selection of young men who shared the same outlook? Not without new purges and new recruitment from the most primitive and unwesternized strata of Russian society, Stalin's approach of the 1930s. In the absence of such a new cataclysm, the bureaucracy drew their replacements more and more from the children of their own class, funneled through the educational pipeline, as manifested by the sharply rising statistics of higher educational attainment among younger members of the political elite. In consequence, the flavor of the intellectual culture was sweetening the well from which came the replenishment of the ruling class. Mikhail Gorbachev himself is the most famous representative of the younger and less hidebound echelons of the political hierarchy, frustrated by the country's manifest stagnation.

The existence of a formidable reform coalition within the bureaucracy was demonstrated upon Brezhnev's death when Andropov successfully challenged the heir apparent Chernenko for the office of General Secretary. To be sure, Andropov's approach to reform was more that of the disciplinarian than of the liberalizer, and the campaign against dissident intellectuals became even more severe during his year. Jews and unofficial peace groups were particularly victimized, and nonconforming cultural figures continued to go into exile abroad. But major changes to the advantage of the intelligentsia were in store. They were suggested by Andropov's denunciation of the dogmatism and sterility of official economics and social science, and the open debates among the specialists that followed. Particularly attractive to the intelligentsia, as many personal reports testified, was the rising young star in the Politburo, Andropov's favorite and protegé Gorbachev.

Andropov's death and replacement by the equally elderly and infirm but emphatically conservative Chernenko in February 1984 came as a rude disappointment to Soviet intellectuals who saw the chances for reform suddenly dashed. Chernenko's brief tenure of the General Secretaryship did slow Andropov's reform momentum, but it quickly became apparent that Gorbachev and the reformers had only made a temporary accommodation with the Chernenko people. They succeeded in elevating their man to the *de facto* second secretaryship and putting him ahead of the candidate most feared by the liberalizers, the former Leningrad party secretary Grigory Romanov. When Chernenko's feeble leadership came to an end with his death in March 1985, Gorbachev was able to win a narrow victory in the Politburo over the representatives of Brezhnevian conservatism.[33] The intelligentsia and the culture it represented had won their best chance since the 1920s to prevail in Russia's national life.

Gorbachev's first year as General Secretary was not particularly dramatic in the cultural sphere. From the time of the April Central Committee plenum in 1985, when he announced the campaign of restructuring and glasnost, to the Twenty-Seventh Party Congress in February–March 1986, Gorbachev's priority was the consolidation of political power, along with appeals in the spirit of Andropov for acceleration, discipline, and sobriety. He removed Romanov and the other top neo-Stalinists from the Politburo, and brought about the highest rate of turnover in the Central Committee that had been seen in 25 years. By the spring of 1986 the reformers seemed firmly in control.

As far as the intelligentsia was concerned, the decisive turning point for Gorbachev came after the Twenty-Seventh Congress. Shaken by the Chernobyl nuclear power disaster and realizing the magnitude of the opposition to his reform campaign that was still firmly rooted lower down in the party and governmental bureaucracy, Gorbachev evidently decided that he must make a political alliance with the intelligentsia. He worked out "a pact—tacit but nonetheless effective," in the words of the *L'Unità* correspondent Giuletto Chiesa,[34] to enlist their support and influence in the cause of reform, in return for the relaxation of political constraints on intellectual freedom. "The problem on the agenda today," Franco Battistrada has pointed out, "is how to pursue a change in cultural approach, in mentality . . . In such an operation, the intelligentsia (in its broadest and most modern sense) cannot play a secondary role, in view of the fact that it has historically fulfilled in Russia and also in the USSR a function, in certain ways unique and irreplaceable, as society's critical conscience. . . ."[35]

In June 1986 Gorbachev bared his concerns about the future of reform in a speech to a special gathering of writers that was widely reported though the official text remains unpublished.[36] Lamenting the resistance to his economic reform, Gorbachev put forth an extraordinary argument for a Soviet leader: "Restructuring is going very badly. We have no opposition. How then can we check up on ourselves? Only through criticism and self-criticism. The main thing is—through glasnost. There cannot be a society without glasnost." Though he hastened to qualify this stance with the familiar Soviet warning that "democratism without a framework is anarchy," Gorbachev made his appeal to the intelligentsia

crystal clear: "The Central Committee needs support. You cannot even imagine how much we need the support of such a force as the writers." He told the founding conference of the Theater Workers' Union in December 1986, "We receive serious support from the intelligentsia, and we expect a great deal from it now, when a struggle is being waged for moral renewal and the attainment of a new qualitative state of society."[37] According to Roy Medvedev, Gorbachev created "a new atmosphere. Late spring and summer of 1986 were characterized, in the cultural life of the USSR, by the strengthening and development of those tendencies of critical renewal and transformation that were linked with the positive changes in the directing group of the CPSU."[38]

In May 1986, a vertible coup d'état took place at the congress of the Cinema Workers' Union, when the delegates removed the old secretary Lyov Kulidzhanov and installed the innovative director Yefrem Klimov. One member of the organization was reported to have shouted, "This is our Poland, our Czechoslovakia."[39] The move put the film union directly at odds with the State Committee on Cinematography (Goskino) under the conservative Filipp Yermash, who was soon removed.

The shake-up in the cinema was followed by a torrent of criticism at the Eighth Writers' Congress in June. Speakers complained of controls that crushed the creative spirit, and called for the publication of long-banned books. Liberal, not-quite-dissident writers such as Yevtushenko and Voznesensky took the lead; declared Voznesensky, "Culture is under attack by spiritual emptiness."[40] As in the film union, the former secretary Georgy Markov was ousted in favor of Vladimir Karpov, editor of *Novyi Mir*, once jailed under Stalin. Similar currents prevailed in the theater when the new Union of Theater Workers was formed in December 1986.

Along with these moves in the main cultural organizations, reformers were installed or encouraged in the editorial direction of a number of newspapers and journals. The weeklies *Moscow News* and *Ogonyok* emerged as regular and enthusiastic organs of reform, setting an example of the illumination of public problems by the press, i.e., glasnost, almost in the Western style. *Novyi Mir's* new editor was the novelist Sergei Zalygin, a non-party member who up to a year or two previously could not even get his own work published. "The press will be the method for democratic control, not control from administration but control with the help of democratic institutions," the noted journalist and theoretician Fyodor Burlatsky (now head of the philosophy section of the Central Committee's Institute of Social Science) said in a press conference at the Reykjavik Summit.[41] Officially the preliminary censorship of books was suspended, except for military secrets.[42] "Our people," said Voznesensky, "have the right to read everything and make their own judgments about everything."[43]

A key aide to Gorbachev in his new approach to the intelligentsia was Alexander Yakovlev, a former cultural functionary and diplomat made head of the Central Committee's Propaganda Department in 1985 and a full member of the Politburo in 1987. Yakovlev became even more explicit than Gorbachev in his promotion of glasnost and his attack on "dogmatism . . . authoritarian thinking elevated to a political, moral, and intellectual principle."[44] Other reformers installed in top ideological positions by 1986 included the new Minister of Culture, V. G. Zakharov (replacing the conservative Pyotr Demichev, who was kicked upstairs to be vice-chairman of the Supreme Soviet); the new head of the Central Committee Cultural Department, Yuri Voronin; the new director of the Institute of Marxism-Leninism, S. L. Smirnov; and the new editor of *Kommunist,* Ivan Frolov (an expert in systems analysis), replacing the conservative-nationalist Richard Kosolapov. The reformist editor of *Sovetskaya Rossiya,* M. F. Nenashev, became chairman of the State Committee for Publishing.

Gorbachev at first drew the line at reopening painful questions of the Soviet past. "If we began to get involved in the past," he told the writers in June 1986, "we would kill off all our energy. We would be hitting the people on the head. And we have to go forward. We will figure out the past. We will put everything in place. But right now we have directed all our energy forward."[45] Nevertheless, glasnost was taken by many writers, by economists, and—with caution—by some historians as an invitation to look again at the unresolved issue of Stalinism. Plans were announced for the publication or performance of long-banned writers, films, and plays, even of Pasternak's *Doctor Zhivago,* and Pasternak himself was posthumously readmitted to the Writers' Union in February 1987. Anatoli Rybakov's novel *Deti Arbata* (Children of the Arbat, serialized in *Druzhba Narodov* in 1987) and Tenghiz Abuladze's film *Pokoyanie* (Repentance, released in Moscow in January 1987) directly or symbolically addressed the terror of the Stalin years, while Mikhail Shatrov's play "The Brest Peace" (*Novyi Mir,* April 1987) brought the Lenin years and Lenin's subsequently purged lieutenants—Trotsky, Bukharin, Zinoviev—back to life more or less objectively.

By early 1987 Gorbachev was evidently persuaded that the spotlight of glasnost could not be withheld from the dark corners of Soviet history. He told the Central Committee at the January 1987 plenum, "The roots of the present situation go back far into the past," and he acknowledged to a meeting of journalists shortly afterwards, "There should be no forgotten names or blank spots in either history or literature. . . . We must not push those who made the revolution into the shadows. . . . It is even more immoral to forget or to pass over in silence entire periods

in the life of the people, who lived, believed and worked under the Party's leadership in the name of socialism. History must be seen as it is. Everything happened, there were mistakes—grave mistakes—but the country moved forward."[46] Historians voiced the need to reconsider the roles of Khrushchev and Brezhnev as well as Stalin, and rumors revived of the impending rehabilitation of Nikolai Bukharin, whose economics of gradualism in the 1920s were fully compatible with Gorbachev's program of restructuring.

One of the most radical aspects of Gorbachev's turn toward the intelligentsia was his attitude towards intellectual emigrés, particularly those who had left the Soviet Union most recently. Andrei Tarkovsky, director of the long withheld historical film "Andrei Rublyov," who went to Italy in 1984 and there directed the highly patriotic "Nostalgia," was hailed in the Soviet press after his death in December 1986, and "Nostalgia" was scheduled to be shown in Moscow. Yuri Liubimov of Taganka Theater fame, and other performers who had defected, including Rostropovich and the dancer Mikhail Baryshnikov, declined invitations to return. The pianist Vladimir Horowitz of the old emigration did visit, to receive a hero's acclaim, and Mark Chagall's paintings were borrowed and exhibited though the painter had by then died.

The most spectacular step in this series of conciliatory moves was the release of Andrei Sakharov from his internal exile in Gorki in December 1986, and his return to an active presence in Moscow. A number of other imprisoned dissidents were released and allowed to emigrate in the early months of 1987, including Anatoly Koryagin, noted for leading the protest against the political abuse of psychiatry. Dissidents both in the Soviet Union and abroad divided in their estimate of all these gestures, some holding that Gorbachev had not really changed the system, others pointing out that he was now saying just what they had been arrested for. Continuing cases of the repression of religious and national-minority activists and the unofficial Trust Group gave grounds to support the skeptics.

The conservative opposition that Gorbachev repeatedly warned about materialized clearly on the cultural front in 1987 in response to all the startling innovations of the previous year. Not surprisingly, the leading spokesman for setting limits to glasnost and decontrol was the number-two man in the party, Yegor Ligachev, widely regarded as the rallying point for political and intellectual conservatism. Ligachev sounded the call for a counterattack in a meeting with the intellectuals of Saratov Province, to whom he conceded the existence of "negative phenomena" and "mistakes of the past," but warned, "To concentrate on the negative alone is only part of the truth." He urged a slowdown in the publication of previously banned works: "Sometimes the assessments given them are exaggerated," and he denounced any steps that would "curtail the leading role of state administration of the cultural sphere." He maintained this stand on later occasions; in June 1987, for example, he cautioned the editorial board of *Sovetskaya Kultura* to insist on more "socialism" and to resist "democratic excesses."[47]

Conservative intellectuals, i.e., those who had won their status as representatives of party control, responded aggressively to Ligachev's initiative. Led by the nationalistic writer Yuri Bondarev, they secured a base in the RSFSR Writers' Union, offsetting the liberal bent of the USSR Writers' Union, and evidently took control of the new Soviet Cultural Foundation. The new editor of *Kommunist*, Frolov, fell in May, an event whose political significance is still unclear. Ivan Laptev, editor of *Izvestia*, addressed the Journalists' Union in June 1987, to warn again of excessively loose interpretations of glasnost and the danger of rejecting seventy years of history. He urged that critical comments be printed with republication of any banned writers. It was in this counter-climate blowing in from the Right that the ultra-nationalist society "Pamyat" (Memory), ostensibly devoted to the preservation of historic buildings, revealed itself as a chauvinistic and anti-Semitic political movement obsessed about Zionist-Masonic plots—in short, a grouping of fascist intellectuals. They suggest an intriguing analogy with the official Slavophiles of the late nineteenth century, more Orthodox than the Tsar.

Gorbachev and his intellectual supporters were obviously aware of the strength and depth of the resistance to reform. The social theorist Butenko, a prominent spokesman for perestroika who had been one of the authors of Khrushchev's utopian program of 1961, recently recalled the fate of reform in those years: "The very same forces that prevented the complete implementation of the decisions of the Twentieth CPSU Congress . . . and to all intents and purposes, interrupted the process of the renewal of our life, do not want changes and are impeding them now, too."[48] Ironically, it is the neo-Stalinists who, in their effort to defend the principle of monolithic party control against the reformers, have divided the party and created more pluralism than the Soviet Union has known since the 1920s.

Since the battle lines were drawn up in 1986, Gorbachev has harped repeatedly on the theme of making reform "irreversible," implying that short of such an attainment the reforms could indeed be reversed. As the playwright Shatrov declared at the theater congress in December 1986, "History is giving us one more chance. And it is our sacred duty not to let this chance slip by, to do everything that is in each person's power to make the process of democratization permanent."[49]

4. Reform from Below or Above?

At the present time it is impossible to foretell the political fate of the Gorbachev leadership and its reform program. But there are circumstances that will not go away, trends in the reality of Soviet society that will sustain and demand political change no matter what. Soviet society, with the entire world, is on the track of modernization and increasing socio-economic complexity, and this makes the intelligentsia, as the bearer of education and expertise, the decisive social element, whatever the institutional context in which it may have to operate. With the passage of three decades since the heyday of Khrushchev's reform efforts, it has become increasingly difficult for Soviet society to function and develop without a free role for the intelligentsia. Life itself to that extent will make Gorbachev's restructuring irreversible.

The basic logic of reform in the Soviet Union in the context of the unfulfilled revolutionary process is more acute than ever. The routinized Stalinism-without-Stalin that the country has endured since the 1960s is an anachronistic perpetuation of the postrevolutionary dictatorship, with all manner of negative consequences. The brain drain of emigration, expulsion, and defection, on the one hand, and on the other the political constriction of the intelligentsia who remained, has meant a colossal wastage of national creativity. While the Soviet Union has nevertheless become a great military and industrial power, its very successes generated new pressure for reform, as the neo-Stalinist system exhausted its potential for further economic and social development, and provoked instead a pervasive state of demoralization and social pathology. It is no longer a joke that the transition phase between socialism and communism is alcoholism. One might say that the critical intelligentsia as a social force for reform was finally joined by the workers and the peasantry, simply in the negative way of refusing to raise their productivity as the progress of the present system requires.

Though hemorrhaging through emigration and oppressed by the political climate, the intelligentsia and its potential audience have still grown in numbers and professional confidence, as the country's impressive establishment of higher education has turned out ever larger numbers of scholars and specialists. At the same time, the bureaucracy has become less certain as a blind anti-reform force, thanks to new blood and new sophistication in its ranks and the recognition that the country's old problems require new solutions. This outlook in the younger echelons of the party apparatus was reflected in the political success of Andropov against Chernenko in 1982 and of Gorbachev against Romanov and Grishin in 1985. Overall there is good reason to judge that the constellation of social forces in the USSR is now much more capable than it was in the 1950s of sustaining the kind of deep reform that would finally return the country to its revolutionary starting point of democratic socialism.

There is, however, a certain irony, familiar in Russian history, to the reform efforts of the current leadership. The initiative for reform has come from the state and the limits of reform are set by the state, implicitly confirming the ultimate power of the political authorities that, when misused, had been responsible for terror or for stagnation. To cure the ills of stagnation under totalitarian controls, the leadership has launched a new effort to revivify society by political command.

One therefore views with some skepticism the aspirations of the leadership toward the "democratization" of the system. The challenge of dismantling Stalinist institutions of political coercion and cultural control has remained far beyond what any of the political leadership seem prepared to contemplate, certainly up to the time when Gorbachev consolidated his position at the Twenty-Seventh Congress. Even a gradual approach to the kind of change that is needed depends too much on the convictions and skill of the reformist leader to overcome the conservative inertia that remains in the bureaucracy.

Though the leadership no doubt regards it as a mere instrument for national progress, what may be the most significant consequence of the reform lies in the mobilization of the resources and enthusiasm of the intelligentsia. The intelligentsia may well emerge from this critical transition period as an independent and irrepressible force to carry Russia truly into the ambit of modern civilization at last. New crises—popular violence, foreign policy embarrassments, renewed trouble among the satellites—could well undercut reform politically, just as happened under Khrushchev. Yet the shape of revolutionary renovation is there for all to see—in the Prague Spring, in some aspects of China's post-Mao reform, in the recent new thinking within the Soviet Union itself, expressed by numerous writers and by the recent rash of independent political clubs. The world will wait with deep interest to see whether the Soviet regime turns at long last in this humane direction.

Notes

1. A. Vasinsky, "Who Permitted the Prohibitions? Polemical Reflections on the Forbiddance Complex," *Izvestia*, December 27, 1986. As in Chapter 4, I have utilized the *Current Digest of the Soviet Press* as a guide to this and other recent Soviet statements.

2. *Pravda*, March 30, 1966.

3. *Ogonyok*, February 9, 1987.

4. The revelation of the identities of "Abram Tertz" and "Nikolai Arzhak" recently became a topic of controversy. Yevtushenko published an article in *Time*

Magazine (February 9, 1987) in which he recounted a meeting with the then Senator Robert Kennedy in the fall of 1966. According to Yevtushenko, Kennedy secretly advised him that the identities of the two writers had been revealed to Soviet intelligence by American agents, for the purpose of provoking the Soviet regime into an act of repression that would discredit it internationally. This account has been disputed by the man who was at that time the CIA's specialist on Soviet dissent, Donald Jameson (*The New Republic,* June 22, 1987). Jameson contends that the American government had neither the knowledge nor the motivation for such a dirty trick, and cites Yevtushenko's interpreter, Professor Albert Todd, that some other unidentified person had made the suggestion about American agents. In any case, the Sinyavsky–Daniel case was a matter of shame which *Moscow News* has now condemned (no. 8, 1987).

5. Deming Brown, *Soviet Russian Literature since Stalin* (Cambridge, England: Cambridge University Press, 1978), pp. 18–19.

6. N. N. Shneidman, *Soviet Literature in the 1970s: Artistic Diversity and Ideological Conformity* (Toronto: University of Toronto Press, 1979), p. 106.

7. Mikhail Suslov, speech to the All-Union Academy of Sciences, "Our Epoch—the Epoch of Celebration of Marxism-Leninism," March 17, 1976, quoted in John Turkevich, "How Science Policy is Formed," *Survey,* XXVI:1 (102, winter 1977–78), p. 115.

8. Cyril R. Black, "New Soviet Thinking," *The New York Times,* November 24, 1978.

9. Alexander Vucinich, *Empire of Knowledge,: The Academy of Sciences of the USSR, 1917–1970* (Berkeley: University of California Press, 1984), pp. 359, 361.

10. See Eugene Zaleski, et al., *Science Policy in the USSR* (Paris: OECD, 1960), p. 571.

11. Jerry F. Hough and Merle Fainsod, *How the Soviet Union is Governed* (Cambridge, Mass.: Harvard University Press, 1979), p. 286.

12. Zaleski, *Science Policy,* p. 561.

13. Zhores Medvedev, *Soviet Science* (New York: Norton, 1978), p. 67.

14. V. G. Afanasiev, *The Scientific and Technological Revolution: Its Impact on Management and Education* (Moscow: Progress Publishers, 1975), p. 294.

15. Vucinich, *Empire of Knowledge,* p. 294.

16. Afanasiev, *The Scientific and Technological Revolution,* p. 295.

17. Zhores Medvedev, *Soviet Science,* pp. 196–198.

18. Afanasiev, *The Scientific and Technological Revolution,* pp. 295–297.

19. Robert W. Campbell, *Soviet Scientific and Technological Education* (McLean, Va.: Science Applications International Corp., 1985), p. 31.

20. Mark Popovsky, *Manipulated Science: The Crisis of Science and Scientists in the Soviet Union Today* (New York: Doubleday, 1979), pp. 142–143.

21. Campbell, *Soviet Scientific Education,* pp. 29, 46.

22. Interview with T. I. Zaslavskaya, *Argumenty i fakty,* March 28–April 3, 1987, p. 5.

23. Campbell, *Soviet Scientific Education,* p. 30.

24. Valentin Turchin, "Scientists among Soviet Dissidents," *Survey,* XXII:12 (fall 1978), p. 87.

25. Erik Hoffmann, "Technology, Values, and Political Power in the Soviet Union: Do Computers Matter?" in Frederic J. Fleron, ed., *Technology and Communist Culture: The Socio-Cultural Impact of Technology under Socialism* (New York: Praeger, 1977) p. 399.

26. Ibid., p. 424.

27. Andrei Amalrik, *Will the Soviet Union Survive until 1984?* (New York: Harper and Row, 1970), p. 15.

28. Quoted in Abraham Rothberg, *The Heirs of Stalin: Dissidence and the Soviet Regime, 1953–1970* (Ithaca, N.Y.: Cornell University Press, 1972), p. 211.

29. Zhores Medvedev, *The Rise and Fall of T. D. Lysenko* (New York: Columbia University Press, 1969).

30. Ludmilla Alexeyeva, *Soviet Dissent: Contemporary Movements for National, Religious, and Human Rights* (Middletown, Conn.: Wesleyan University Press, 1985), pp. 293–294.

31. Ibid., pp. 344–345.

32. Interview with A. I. Volodin, *Pravda*, March 10, 1987.

33. Earlier rumors of a five-to-four decision were confirmed in an article by the playwright Mikhail Shatrov, *Ogonyok*, January 26, 1986.

34. Roy Medvedev and Giulietto Chiesa, *L'Urss che cambia* (The Changing USSR, Rome: Riuniti, 1987), p. 266.

35. Franco Battistrada, "Trasparenza si ma anche sul passato" (Openness, Yes, but Also on the Past), *Rinascita*, January 17, 1987, p. 34.

36. Notes of Gorbachev's speech circulated in samizdat. See "Beseda chlenov SP SSSR s M. S. Gorbachevym" (Talk of Members of the USSR Writers' Union with M. S. Gorbachev), Arkhiv Samizdata, No. 5785. Excerpts were published in *L'Unità* and *La Republica*, October 7, 1986. A partial summary appeared in *Pravda*, June 21, 1986.

37. *Pravda*, December 15, 1986.

38. Roy Medvedev, "Il secondo, contrastato disgelo" (The Second, Contrasting Thaw), *Rinascita*, November 8, 1986, p. 6.

39. *Newsweek*, June 9, 1986.

40. *Literaturnaya Gazeta*, July 2, 1986.

41. Radio Liberty Reports, No. 396/86, p. 4.

42. Roy Medvedev, "Il secondo disgelo," p. 7.

43. *Literaturnaya Gazeta*, February 25, 1987.

44. A. N. Yakovlev, speech at meeting of intelligentsia in Dushanbe, *Pravda*, April 10, 1987.

45. Arkhiv Samizdata, No. 5785, p. 5.

46. *Pravda*, January 17 and February 14, 1987.

47. *Pravda*, March 5, 1987; *Sovetskaya Kultura*, July 7, 1987.

48. Interview with Anatoly Butenko, *Moskovskaya Pravda*, May 7, 1987.

49. *Pravda*, December 7, 1986.

7

The Revolutionary Legacy

Zdeněk Mlynař, Ideological Secretary in the Prague Spring government of 1968 and Gorbachev's university roommate in the early 1950s, recently remarked perceptively that it would be politically risky for the cause of reform in the Soviet Union to reopen questions of the past.[1] Mikhail Gorbachev started his regime saying the same thing. Yet no genuine and durable reform of the present Soviet system can be accomplished without a fundamental reexamination of the relation of this system to the historical past that generated it, including its origins in the Revolution of 1917.

It is still not possible to judge the Soviet system without reference to the revolutionary process that began almost seventy years ago. The Soviet Union today represents a very late stage in the typical life history of a revolution. It is the outcome of a series of political convulsions, beginning with the liberal revolution of February 1917, and continuing with the radical revolution of Lenin in October, the violent and utopian adventure of War Communism, the Thermidorean consolidation of the New Economic Policy of the 1920s, and the Bonapartist postrevolutionary dictatorship of Stalin (including its phases of radical reconstruction, 1929–1934, and conservative consolidation, 1934–1939).

Stalin's postrevolutionary synthesis of revolutionary rhetoric, traditional values, and totalitarian methods, his amalgam of socialism, nationalism, and bureaucracy, remains the basis of the present Soviet political system. But this existing order may not be the final phase in the Russian revolutionary process. Certain historical parallels with the classic revolutions of European history suggest an as yet unrealized potential for profound reform in the Soviet system. Seventeenth-century England, after civil war, the Puritan Commonwealth, and the Stuart Restoration, turned back to the first principles of the parliamentary revolution in the "Glorious Revolution" of 1688. Similarly, France, after the Great Revolution, the Terror, the Napoleonic era, and the Bourbon Restoration, returned in the Revolution of 1830 to the constitutional ideas of 1789.

In general, no revolutionary society has rested indefinitely in the grip of its counterrevolutionary sequel. It appears that the revolutionary experience is not complete until the nation has an opportunity to overthrow the postrevolutionary dictatorship (or the restored monarchy) and accomplish what I term the "moderate revolutionary revival." This last phase recaptures the early principles of the revolution, but avoids the extremist fanaticism that carried it into subsequent violent and despotic behavior. Similar outcomes have manifested themselves where the postrevolutionary dictatorship took the form of right-wing totalitarianism, which in Germany gave way after the destruction of Hitlerism to a revival of the Weimar regime in the Federal Republic, and in Spain after the death of Franco in 1975 to a restoration of the democracy of 1931–1936.

The logic of the revolutionary process manifested in all these historical situations suggests that a similar final step is due to take place sooner or later in Soviet Russia. In this case historical parallelism would call for throwing off the legacy of Stalinism and returning to the original hopes and enthusiasm of 1917, based on a democratic, multi-party, decentralized, participatory socialism. This was the ultra-democratic Russia of the early soviets, hailed even by Lenin in his *State and Revolution*, but overwhelmed by one-party dictatorship after the hope of a government of all socialist parties was aborted by the Bolsheviks' violent seizure of power.

The possibility of a return to revolutionary beginnings in the Soviet Union is not just a matter of hypothetical historical reasoning. The real pressure for such a renovation, based on the rejection of the Stalinist system, has been demonstrated time and again by attempts at reform in Eastern Europe—in Poland and in Hungary in 1956, in Czechoslovakia in 1968, and again in Poland in 1980. In a more qualified way it has figured in Yugoslavia since the early 1950s and in China under Deng Xiao-ping.

For Russia itself the first opportunity for the moderate revolutionary revival was the death of Stalin. The cultural thaw and Khrushchev's de-Stalinization campaign were important steps toward actualizing this possibility. But Khrushchev failed to attack the Stalinist system of rule, in distinction to its excesses, and did not develop an independent social base for reform, such as the English aristocracy provided in 1688 or the French bourgeoisie in 1830. The potential was there, in the form of the cultural and technical intelligentsia, but these elements had neither the independence nor the organization to influence the party or resist the police once their personal patron was unseated. Khrushchev left intact the postrevolutionary dictatorship, moderated and modernized to some extent, discredited in the outside world, but unchanged in its essentials at home. Now in the 1980s, following the deaths of Brezhnev and his immediate successors, and the accession to power of an altogether new generation, there is an historic opportunity once again to rid the country of its postrevolutionary burden, and recover the genuine inspiration of 1917 and its socialism with a human face.

This is exactly what was demanded in the remarkable samizdat manifesto of November 1985, "To the Citizens of the USSR," issued by the self-styled "Movement of Socialist Renewal" in Leningrad. Demanding both economic reforms and political democratization, the group asserted, "Having secured the full and final victory of socialism, the dictatorship of the proletariat has fulfilled its historic mission, from the point of view of its internal development, and has ceased to be necessary in the USSR."[2]

Is Gorbachev a leader with the intention or the ability to mobilize the available social forces and carry out the kind of reform that the logic of the revolution requires? In his speeches calling for perestroika and glasnost he has made it plain that he is dedicated to fundamental change of some sort. "I would equate the word restructuring with the word revolution," he declared at Khabarovsk in July 1986.[3] His revolutionary steps have ranged from permitting the election of liberal literary and film leaders, to the release of Andrei Sakharov from internal exile. Mingling with workers at Krasnodar in September 1986, Gorbachev asserted, "If we now retreated from what we have begun, our people would be greatly disappointed. And that would affect everything. We can't allow this to happen."[4]

The ascendancy of Gorbachev has created a situation closely paralleling the era of Khrushchev. This time the tensions between the reformist intelligentsia and the anachronistic party bureaucracy are even more pronounced. Judging by his extraordinary remarks to the writers in June 1986, Gorbachev is quite conscious of the similar alignment of forces. He called frankly upon the intelligentsia to help him offset the inertia of the "administrative layer—the apparatus of the ministries, the party apparatus—that does not want changes" and thereby clear the way for "restructuring" Soviet society. "Society is ripe for a sharp turn [*povorot*]," he is reported to have said. "If we retreat, society will not agree to a return. We have to make the process irreversible. If not us, then who? If not now, when?" "Our enemies," he concluded, only fear our democratization. "They write about the apparatus that broke Khrushchev's neck, and about the apparatus that will break the neck of the new leadership."[5]

Ironically, the shift from Stalin's despotism to the present collective leadership has made it more difficult for a reform-minded leader to command change from above. The relationship of the General Secretary to the representatives of the bureaucracy in the Politburo and the Central Committee has become one of mutual vulnerability, illustrated first by the fall of Malenkov in 1955, then by Khrushchev's narrow escape in 1957, and subsequently by the fall of the latter in 1964. Brezhnev never ventured to threaten the interests of the bureaucracy. To be sure, Gorbachev has been able to use his new authority to accelerate the generational renovation of the bureaucracy begun by Andropov in 1982–1983. In the Central Committee installed by the Twenty-Seventh Party Congress, 44% of the members were new. Yet if the leader tries to move too far or too fast to change policy or personnel in the name of reform, and if the Politburo and Central Committee can coalesce in time, he can be removed and replaced. Second Secretary Ligachev, a protegé of Andropov who is ten years older than Gorbachev, has already offered hints that he could be a rallying point for the conservatives if the time comes.

The prospects for a reform that would consummate the moderate revolutionary revival in Russia are further limited by historical circumstances. Thanks to Stalin's postrevolutionary assimilation of the Russian past into the Soviet present, the system still embodies the long Russian tradition of centralized, bureaucratic, and despotic government, endowed by its exclusive official faith with what Gorbachev himself has condemned as an "infallibility complex."[6] As a secret dissident said to me in Moscow a few years ago, "The trouble with the Soviet Union is that we still have too much Orthodoxy." The question is whether any reform, any new leadership, even a change of regime, could alter the way in which Russia has been ruled for centuries and continues to be ruled. Perhaps the spirit of 1917 represented such a radical break from the Russian past that it could not be successfully revived and sustained even now.

While politically the Russian historical legacy impedes reform, economically the same legacy makes reform imperative. The Stalinist economic system was a premature imposition on a relatively backward society where capitalism had not had the opportunity to develop the country's industrial potential fully. Even more serious, though not so widely appreciated, was the fact that capitalism had not yet accomplished the concentration and modernization of the country's petty-bourgeois economic sectors—agriculture, trade, and services—that might have made them ready for socialization. Abrupt nationalization in 1918 and its reaffirmation along with the collectivization of agriculture when Stalin ended the NEP in 1929 set these immature sectors back to an extent that they have not even yet recovered from. This error of premature socialization of pre-capitalist sectors has sooner or later been recognized and addressed in most Communist countries that have been sufficiently independent of the Soviet mode (Yugoslavia, Poland, Hungary, China).

Steps in the same direction are now being hinted at in the Soviet Union itself, notably by the law of November 19, 1986, legalizing family enterprise.

While the Soviet economy in the sectors noted suffers from revolutionary prematurity, in the industrial sector it suffers from the political anachronism of the Russian tradition of centralism, reinstituted in an extreme form in the Stalinist command economy. The cost of this in the inhibition of initiative and innovation is finally being recognized today in the Soviet Union, as economic growth stagnates and the technological gap vis-à-vis the West steadily widens. The well-known "Novosibirsk Report" of 1983 by the sociologist Tatiana Zaslavskaya put the blame on "the lagging of the system of production relations, and hence of the mechanism of state management of the economy which is its reflection, behind the level of development of the productive forces." State management as practiced since the 1930s, Zaslavskaya observed, reflected "the predominance of administrative over economic methods, of centralization over decentralization."[7] Gorbachev has warned (in the Khabarovsk speech), "There will be no progress if we seek answers to new questions in the economy and in technology in the experience of the 1930s, the 1940s, the 1950s, or even of the 1960s and the 1970s."[8] (He conspicuously left open the 1920s and the NEP for lessons in decentralization.) Here is the front line in the current battle between the Gorbachevian modernizers and the Brezhnevian (and Andropovite) conservatives. The issue will not disappear no matter what happens to the current reformist leadership.

Hovering over all aspects of the reform question, political and economic, there is still the question of the relationship of the Soviet regime to its professed ideology and its actual history. As a postrevolutionary regime still clinging to a revolutionary mythology for its legitimacy, the Soviet regime has been compelled to control all channels of cultural and intellectual expression that might convey doubts about the legitimizing tie with the revolutionary past. This need, reinforced by Stalin's personal mania, has been the basis for the whole system of stultifying dictation maintained since his time over all forms of artistic creation, historical investigation, and speculative thought. It is as though an entire nation were subjected to a pervasive historical neurosis, demanding repression or mythologizing of the regime's own record to fit the psychological needs of a defensive and anxious ruling elite. The price paid by the nation in lost creativity and intellectual apathy has been inestimable.

None of this is necessary. It is possible, as the West European Left has shown, to rethink one's ideological heritage and escape from the burden of historical and philosophical dogmatism. Referring to Gorbachev's "lesson of truth" pronounced at the Twenty-Seventh Congress,

Giuseppe Boffa commented, "We Italian Communists have been trying to tell this truth all these years."[9] I would go even further. The time has come, as a logical imperative if not as a political possibility, for the Soviet Union itself to recognize that, in the sensational words of Enrico Berlinguer, "The propulsive force that had its origin in the October Revolution has become exhausted."[10]

Reform in Soviet Russia in the sense of a moderate revolutionary revival would not mean the repudiation of socialism. Socialism, in its essence as the overthrow of the power of private property in human relations, is the soul of the Russian Revolution, even though it may appear to many critics as a lost soul. What reform would require, as Mlynař points out, is a reconsideration of the bureaucratic, centralist, Russian-style socialism that has been maintained ever since Stalin's time as if it were the only conceivable expression of the ideal. Such a reconsideration is clearly the direction of Gorbachev's current efforts, exemplified in his economic reforms, his espousal of glasnost, and his call to breathe life into the local soviets.

There is ample precedent for an anti-bureaucratic socialism in the history of the Communist movement—in the Workers' Opposition in Russia in 1921, in Yugoslavia in a limited way since 1950, in China in diverse ways both during and since the Cultural Revolution—not to mention the West European New Left of 1968. Santiago Carrillo suggested in *Eurocommunism and the State*, "The progress of the socialist movement in the developed capitalist countries may help Soviet society and the Soviet Communists to go beyond that type of state . . . which . . . tends to place itself above its own society and above the societies of other countries, a type of state which tends toward coercion through a series of objective and subjective factors, . . . and make progress in transforming it into a real working people's democracy."[11] In other words, the traditional Soviet notion that the first socialist country shows the way to all others must be reversed.

As a practical matter, despite the exhortations of the European Left, fundamental reform based on a true return to revolutionary beginnings may remain a political impossibility in the Soviet Union, since it requires just that reconsideration of the past that arouses more political resistance and thereby makes the success of reform less likely. But there are underlying circumstances that have not yet had their full effect on the surface of Soviet reality—the pressures and needs of a modern society, the tension between the regime and its revolutionary origins, the impatience of a new generation of leadership. China over the last decade has illustrated how quickly and surprisingly a great nation in the Marxist-Leninist tradition may change under the pressure of such circumstances. To be sure, the more applicable precedents for reform offered by Eastern

Europe have had discouraging outcomes, thanks to Soviet intervention. But if any comparable reform should be attempted within the Soviet Union itself, there is no one to intervene against it.

Notes

1. Zdeněk Mlynař, "Il crocevia della riforma politica" (The Crossroads of Political Reform), *Rinascita*, 8 November 1986.

2. "K grazhdanam Sovetskogo Soyuza," November 21, 1985, Arkhiv Samizdata, no. 5724.

3. Gorbachev, speech at a conference of the Khabarovsk Territory Party Organization, July 31, 1986, *Pravda*, August 2, 1986.

4. Gorbachev, talk with citizens in Krasnodar, September 18, 1986, *Pravda*, September 19, 1986.

5. "Beseda chlenov SP SSSR s M. S. Gorbachevym" (Talk of Members of the USSR Writers' Union with M. S. Gorbachev), Arkhiv Samizdata, n. 7585, pp. 1, 6.

6. Gorbachev at the Twenty-Seventh Congress of the CPSU, reported by Giuseppe Boffa in *L'Unità*, April 2, 1986.

7. "The Novosibirsk Report," *Survey*, XXXVIII:1 (spring 1984), pp. 88–89.

8. Gorbachev, speech of July 31, 1986.

9. *L'Unità*, March 8, 1986.

10. Enrico Berlinguer, statement on Italian television, December 15, 1981.

11. Santiago Carrillo, *Eurocommunism and the State* (Westport, Conn.: Lawrence Hill, 1978), p. 172.

Index

135